MICHAEL PODOLNY'S

SHORTCUT TO SECURITY

Make Your Business Worth More to You©

by Michael Podolny

with Joel Eisenberg

PRAISE FOR MICHAEL PODOLNY and
THE PODOLNY METHOD©

JOHN BUFFETT
B & H WHOLESALE

We started using Mike in the spring of '05 due to mounting frustrations between our family members. The frustrations stemmed from differences of opinion as to the direction of our company. Mike's relatively simple method enabled us to devise an effective business plan that all of our family members agreed to and supported. He remains a most trusted advisor and a crucial factor in our success.

LOREN ELLIOT
CORPORATE TRAINER

The Podolny Method© is a revolution, and Mike Podolny's Shortcut to Security a revelation. This new tome illustrates practical, sensible business strategies that any entrepreneur could utilize. It is one of the very best books of the year.

DAVID GOULD
CEO, THERMOPRO, LLC

I highly recommend Mike Podolny and his Podolny Method© for any small business owner in most any circumstance.

STEVE SAUNDERS
PRESIDENT
IRON MOUNTAIN MEDIA

Mike Podolny has been utilizing his widely acclaimed The Podolny Method© on small to large business for many years to help them achieve their financial goals. Now, finally, he shares his groundbreaking strategies with you. Mike Podolny's Shortcut to Security will surely become one of the preeminent finance books of its era. Thank you Mike!

BILL SCOTT
DION'S PIZZA

Mike's method is simple, straightforward, and energetic. It certainly worked well for us.

JOHN R. SHELTON
MARKETSPACE FINANCIAL, INC.
Thank you for all the work you have done for MarketSpace Financial, Inc. over the years. Your patience, guidance, and discipline have put us on the right track to achieving our goals in business and in life.

SAM ZAIDSPINER
SLINGSHOT PRODUCT DEVELOPMENT GROUP
We have acted on many of the key findings that resulted from The Podolny Method© and from the monthly review sessions. We have dramatically improved our business structure, and we are building momentum on a daily basis. Most importantly, my week is more efficient and focused, so I am spending less time on weekends and evenings working and more time with my family.

GINNY BERGER
ACC DENTAL CONSULTANTS, INC.
"The Podolny Group has been instrumental in growing and developing my company, ACC Consultants Inc. The qualified team from Podolny Group really understands our purpose and has helped guide and drive us to excellence. They have been successful in understanding our culture and helping us to meet financial goals while aligning them with our team and the way we enjoy working together. I would highly recommend The Podolny Group to anyone, especially those who may not know where they want to go with their business - as The Podolny Group will help you find your way."

CINDY MAUCHLY
PRESIDENT, SANTA FE CUSTOM WORKS
"The Podolny Group is different. I was feeling stuck, a slave to the business I had created. My goal in engaging with Michael and his team was to position myself and my business to have choices. We started by looking at what was right with the business, and then explored what could be changed in order for me to reach my goals. Through their collective insights, expertise, experience and coaching I have changed the way I view my role, my future and my business as a whole. Specifically, as a team, we looked at the areas of the business that were not serving my goals. One by one we addressed these areas, made systematic changes and the results came very quickly. As a result of working with The Podolny Group my business has matured, my choices have grown and I am a different business owner today than I was a year ago."

MICHAEL PODOLNY'S

SHORTCUT TO SECURITY

Make Your Business Worth More to You©

by Michael Podolny

with Joel Eisenberg

MICHAEL PODOLNY'S
SHORTCUT TO SECURITY
Make Your Business Worth More to You©

Original material Copyright 2008
by Michael Podolny
ISBN 1-881249-48-4

Printed in the United States of America

Published by Business Strategies
1849 Tramway Terrace Lp.
Albuquerque, NM 87122

First Printing

Published in the United States, Canada, and the United Kingdom

Address all queries
The Podolny Group, Inc.
2108 White Cloud NE
Albuquerque, NM 87112
(505) 856-2646
www.podolny.com

DEDICATION

This book is dedicated to the thousands of private business owners who pour their hearts and souls into their businesses. Are all these people wonderful human beings working for the benefit of their employees, customers, and suppliers—not to mention mankind in general? No, of course not. As in all walks of life, there are the good and the bad.

But over the course of my three decades of working with owners, I have found that the majority want to do the right thing and often work on behalf of their stakeholders—to the detriment of their own well-being. It is my hope that this book will enable those who create employment, who contribute to their communities, and who are in large part responsible for the economic well-being of our country, to achieve the personal success that is fully within their grasp.

ACKNOWLEDGEMENTS

I would like to acknowledge the assistance of Joel Eisenberg. Joel has been much more than a writer; he has helped me understand how to integrate this book project with the bigger vision I have had for my business and my life. I would also like to thank Scott Kriloff and Deborah Jackson of his staff for their editorial expertise.

A special thanks to David Sahd, my first marketing guru, who pushed me to write my first book, who oversaw the development of The Podolny Group E-Letter—Make Your Business Serve You—who pushed me to develop my website, and who has choreographed the publishing now of this book.

I also want to thank all the mentors I have had throughout my life, and those people who gave me breaks earlier in my career, without whom I would never have developed the skills necessary to do the work that I do. I especially want to thank my father, whose contacts led to my first job in banking; the late Jerry Harris and his partner Steve Goldsmith, who gave me my first break into the mergers/acquisitions business; and Hank Kelly of the Albuquerque law firm of Sutin, Thayer & Browne, who had the confidence to refer me to his many contacts in New Mexico when no one there knew me.

I want to thank all of my associates in The Podolny Group, but especially Frank Huybrechts, Joseph Sutton, and Craig Dill, who were, in many ways, the guinea pigs for the development of my business.

My special appreciation goes to Alexis Podolny—who has a unique insight into me and the travails of growing The Podolny Group—for her skillful and ingenious artwork.

Thanks to Leslie Crosby, Linda Huybrechts and David Sahd for their efforts editing this book.

Finally, I want to thank my parents for the core values that have been expressed in the values of my method and my business, and for their help, both psychological and financial, during the most difficult periods of my life; my three daughters, Stephanie, Lisa, and Alexis, for enduring all the pains of my personal development; and last but not least, my wife Gloria, whose patience and support has been unending.

A NOTE FROM THE PUBLISHER

Business Strategies, the publisher of this book, has itself benefited from the advice and guidance of Michael Podolny. That is one reason we can confidently claim that Shortcut to Security – Make Your Business Worth More to You© will give you a roadmap for increasing the value of your company.

But the book offers much more than that. Michael Podolny hasn't just outlined a step-by-step process. He has developed sound reasoning for taking certain actions and described how to implement executable action plans.

Podolny has helped hundreds of business owners turn their enterprises into wealth-building machines. He understands that the financial, operational, marketing and other aspects of running a successful company never stand alone. Therefore, when he encourages strategies in one area of the business, the associated action items take into account other important elements of business management.

His approach creates a symphony of strategy, planning, action, implementation and, most importantly, results!

Once you have finished reading this book, you will have a comprehensive understanding of a complex issue that Podolny has distilled into easily digestible segments. That makes moving forward with making your business more valuable less daunting. It also makes it simple to put into action.

David M. Sahd
Publisher

AUTHOR'S NOTE

Building, maintaining and ultimately *selling* a successful business is the entrepreneur's dream. Yet it is estimated that eighty percent of all businesses fail and will not be around after five years. *Eighty percent!* Of the remaining twenty percent that do survive, however, few of those owners will create enough wealth by the time they are done with their business to support the lifestyle they enjoyed while *in* the business. Sobering statistics, to be sure, but one for which there are numerous *avoidable* reasons.

Firstly, many budding entrepreneurs who enter into a business for the first time, or even veterans for that matter, simply don't have a clue as to what they're doing.

They have or have been presented with an appealing scenario, and they jump at the opportunity to get involved. Yet do they really have the knowledge of what it takes to successfully deliver the service, or to sell the product? Would you have this knowledge?

How about this: Perhaps, there is no market for their product. Have you ever been involved in a business where you jumped in, and regretted it later? Did you do your diligence beforehand, or was the decision to enter into this business an *impulsive* one. Like television and billboard advertising that caters to the emotions, or the gut, did you rush to get involved in the *next big thing* because you studied up on your prospect, or due to the chord that was struck? In other words, was your decision intellectually or emotionally-based?

Consider this: Two billboards representing competing beers. One billboard illustrates a photo of a lovely young woman in a pink bikini, holding a bottle of her favorite ale as the beach beckons behind her. For the viewer, or *voyeur* in this case, an emotional chord has most definitely been struck. The other billboard, meanwhile, showcases a stick figure also holding a bottle, also standing in the stead of the beach.

Which beer would you be most apt to buy?

Many fledgling entrepreneurs get involved in business similarly--on impulse. Here are the drawbacks: Maybe they have not gone through the process of finding out whether anybody really does spend money on this kind of thing. Or, relative to the prior example, they may not understand how to sell whatever it is that they're selling. *I think there's a market for this* is not good enough. Good intentions don't pay the mortgage. *I'm going to represent this product and get it out there for the world's benefit.* But do you really understand how to grow the business to bring the clients in?

Sometimes small businesses start strongly but suffer major growing pains as they add staff. The minute they start adding people, they start having problems in terms of quality in what they are doing. Poor management has been responsible for killing off more potentially successful companies than just about anything else. What about *you?* You picked up this book for a reason. Have you hired the best people for your business, or did your inexperienced family member come cheaper? How many new owners have you known who start spending all the business receipts as they start coming in without regard to taxes, bills, expenses, etc.?

The bottom line: In order to enable your business to pay for your eventual financial independence, your business needs to be properly managed. You *must* understand the difference between *gross* and *net* income. Believe me, many do not.

So, what have we learned so far? If you're honest with yourself, you can admit right now that most of what I have written to this point really is not groundbreaking at all!

In fact, earning the income, prudently managing the income and subsequently having your business pay for your retirement is *not* rocket science. Indeed, there is a *shortcut to security.* And it's all common sense. The elements of managing your financial future don't have to be a mystery.

Welcome to my course …

PART ONE

The Educated Entrepreneur

CHAPTER ONE

Why a Comfortable Retirement
Is *Not* a Given Result of Business Ownership

You build a bicycle. You take it for a test drive. Everything is good, the bicycle works fine. You made a smart investment, an investment in your health, guaranteed to keep you physically fit for many a year—assuming, of course, that you follow the rules and utilize your new equipment on a regular basis. If you do, the returns will be immeasurable.

Why do so many individuals go into business for themselves, especially without a business plan or a plan for achieving financial independence? Why do so few succeed and so many fail?

You start a business from nothing. You receive your first checks and are convinced that you will almost certainly be able to live well for the next twenty, thirty, or forty years. After all, you are already getting paid for your efforts. Good job! Your plans have been validated; all you have to do now is keep up the hard work. But then, the bills start coming in—rent, insurance, payables—and your taxes are due in a week! Suddenly, you ask yourself, *What's happened to my income?*

The short answer, which may appear obvious on the surface, but in reality is not nearly so simple, is that *a comfortable retirement is in no way a given result of business ownership*. Then why do so many individuals go into business for themselves, especially without a business plan or a plan for achieving financial independence? Why do so few succeed and so many fail? Fortunately, my experiences led me to write this book. Unfortunately, my experiences led me to write this book...

> *A business owner drags himself into work. He is tired and frustrated. It would be so much easier, he thinks, if I just had a job. I could go in, work forty hours, go home, and not worry about making the payroll, paying the bills, getting the work out, or keeping the government off my back.*

> *Another business owner is sitting in her office. She is upset...again. She has put years of work into her business. Her company has become one of the leaders in its market area. The business is profitable and successful, but the owner has just had a fight with her partner (for the umpteenth time) over company policy and direction. It wasn't supposed to be this way. Once her business had reached this level, she was supposed to be able to enjoy it.*

> *A third business owner is racking his brain, trying to solve a problem. After years of struggling, his company has reached a point where he knows it is ready to go to another level. Even so, that potential seems to be just out of his grasp. He can't quite get the formula right despite trying numerous alternatives.*

How many business owners do you know who are truly happy with their work? Chances are, very few. Then why do people go into business for themselves in the first place? What is the allure of discarding the security of a nine-to-five job to risk the relative unknown of entrepreneurship? There are several reasons:

- **Independence** – not having to answer to someone else
- **Wealth** – the opportunity to be more than a wage slave
- **Self-determination** – becoming the master of one's own fate

- **Ego satisfaction** – the chance to express one's competitive nature
- **Accomplishment** – the satisfaction of seeing something come to fruition because of one's own efforts

Yet, it has been my observation that what the majority of business owners experience is actually very different:

- **Frustration** – the feeling that their efforts are constantly being thwarted rather than leading to accomplishment
- **Risk** – having one's wealth and well-being subject to loss
- **Enslavement** – a situation where the owner feels that the business controls his or her life
- **Worry** – the business and its circumstances are constantly weighing on the business owner's mind

> *Frustration, Risk, Enslavement, and Worry are not preordained. You can—and indeed should— achieve independence, wealth, self-determination, ego satisfaction, and accomplishment from owning a business.*

The above conditions of Frustration, Risk, Enslavement, and Worry, though, are *not* pre-ordained. You can—and indeed should—achieve independence, wealth, self-determination, ego satisfaction, and accomplishment from owning a business. But what are steadfastly required to achieve these positive outcomes are *new perspectives*.

In that spirit…

> *A group of blind men are seated in a row. There is a single animal in front of them. The first person is asked to stand and feel the animal. He touches smooth, thick tusks and states right away that the animal is an elephant. The*

*second person feels only the legs and argues that the
animal must be tall and thin. The third disagrees, saying
the creature is long and broad. The last feels only the tail
and insists he's feeling a snake. The bottom line is that
each man only grasps a very small piece of the whole, and
unless they get somebody to pull all those pieces together
into a Big Picture, there is no way to figure out exactly
what that whole is.*

Myth: *The majority of business owners develop a sense of
"foresight" that enables them to analyze the Big Picture
before they assume the risk of self-employment.*

Reality: *Most business owners are "short-sighted" and
ill-prepared to take on the risks of business ownership.*

This problem is not always the fault of the entrepreneur,
however.

Here's a disturbing question—how many of today's public
schools even teach the concept of balancing a checkbook? Where
does this fit in with the concepts of *algebra* or *geometry*? In the
same line of thinking, how many pre-college students are taught
budgeting, from either their schools or their parents? Is anyone
really taught about credit cards, their benefits and their dangers?
How about even the most *basic* financial knowledge, such as
opening a passbook savings account? Is there a class in high school
that teaches you how to calculate the payments of a new car, so
as to determine whether you can afford it? This country is based
on entrepreneurship, yet where did *you* learn the tenets of being a
business owner? *Was there a business owner boot camp for you?* Were
you taught by your parents…by anybody?

Or, like most, were you self-taught?

Let's run with this. How many people do you know who love
their job, are crazy about their boss, and jump out of bed every
morning motivated to go to work? Do *you* feel lucky to go to work
each day?

For most people, the thought of negotiating the Big Picture
and having to learn and develop the skills necessary for successful

business ownership is overwhelming. As a result... most do not even try. They work for someone else and retire with a memory and a great deal of stress as to how they will pay their bills.

So why then do most business owners who *do* take on these challenges still have problems achieving an acceptable end? Though it's not rocket science, the skills necessary for successful business ownership are not generally taught in our schools. However, if you learn the rules, you will come to understand that there is definitely a pathway to success, a *Shortcut to Security*. Like the allegory of the four blind men above, there is no individual component that is the magic key. None of the individual pieces of the picture is all that challenging or difficult to learn for the motivated entrepreneur.

You must consider the *whole*, the Big Picture. If you don't, your business is dead before it begins.

So now that we understand each other...let's fast-forward. You are excited about your new startup. And why wouldn't you be? You shouldn't be in business if you are anything less than 100 percent committed.

However, let's discuss those individuals who represent the bulk of these brand-new startups. For one, they have never owned a business before. They will likely mismanage their money, especially at the beginning, because they will confuse *gross revenues* with *net income*. The checks start coming in, and they suddenly need a new car. Or a new television. And *then* they remember the business bills only later.

Generalizations? Perhaps, but again—80 percent of all businesses fail, so I feel justified continuing with the following three simple lessons:

THE STARTUP
LESSON ONE

New business owners typically misunderstand, or otherwise under-estimate, the payables cycle. They do the work, they bill their clients, and they have enough money remaining for a limited payroll, with just enough after that to pay some of their vendors...but now the money is not coming in fast enough to meet the following month's bills. Their first thought is typical: *I'll catch up as soon as more money comes in.* This cycle, in fact, tends to perpetuate and get worse as a company grows and hires new employees.

> **Myth:** *Company growth is the key to success.*
>
> **Reality:** *Company growth can indeed be the key to success… so long as you prepare to meet the demands of a larger business, and <u>understand the cost of growth versus the time it takes to get a return from growth.</u>*

Frequently, a new business entity, usually started with a minimum of capital, will do fine in the first year or two. But as it begins to achieve some success and starts to grow, it risks outstripping its capital base. Then the owner finds he must parcel out the money that comes in *(I'll pay this bill. I won't pay that bill.)*— initiating a dangerous downward spiral that can quickly prove disastrous.

There is an immutable rule for business—as a business starts to grow and picks up its rate of growth, **it uses capital**. This is exceedingly important to understand. *Not understanding this one point has cost innumerable business owners the returns they were looking for, and even cost them their businesses!* **Growth uses capital**.

The opposite is also true. A mature business that is not growing rapidly (particularly one that is in a relatively mundane industry and does not require a heavy amount of reinvestment in order to keep it in a position of stability) may be able to be perfectly healthy. *And, more importantly, it can spin off surplus capital…a prime source of potential wealth for the business owner.* **Stability leads to the ability to produce surplus capital.**

Here's an illustration of how growing or not growing can impact a business and its owners:

I once worked with a company in the restaurant business. When I started working with them, they had eight restaurants. The owners' strategic plan was to open an additional new restaurant every year, for five years, and then sell the business. As part of my analysis, we looked at this growth plan and determined how much it would cost the owners to open each new restaurant. Then came a key question:

IBITDA is an acronym for **Income Before Interest, Taxes, Depreciation, and Amortization.** *It is something every business owner should take the time to comprehend, because for anybody who has a business of any size (especially for any business with more than $3 million in sales), IBITDA is going to be the primary basis upon which the business will be evaluated. The value of a business, its enterprise value, is the product of IBITDA and an appropriate multiple. If you don't understand IBITDA, get to know it. A huge portion of the value of your business depends on it. Reality check: Fewer than 10 percent of the companies I deal with have any clue as to the importance of IBITDA, or even what it means. For more about IBITDA and business valuation, see Chapter Twelve.*

How are you going to pay for these restaurants?. The answer was: "We're going to borrow the money from our bank." So into the analysis went the amount of the loan for each new location, and the time period required to repay that loan.

Then we prepared a financial projection. At first blush, this showed that with the addition of the projected sales from the proposed new restaurant locations, the projected valuation of the business was increased, because the projected cash flow (IBITDA—Income Before Interest, Taxes, Depreciation, and Amortization—see sidebar) of the business increased substantially.

However, then we accounted for the debt (the amount that was going to be left on the balance sheet), taking into account the amount needed for each restaurant and the payback period we had used in our assumptions. There was going to be a lot of debt left in the company. And since *debt is taken out of the proceeds of a business sale in the vast majority of cases,* we subtracted that from our projected valuation. This substantially reduced the amount the owners would have received. The net income the owners were looking at was just above $3 million.

At the same time, we calculated a separate no-expansion scenario. *What would the situation look like if we didn't open any additional restaurants over the five-year period?* In that scenario, we could pay off what little existing debt remained, and the scenario started generating surplus cash. Just as you subtract the outstanding debt balance from the value on a sale of a business, *you add any surplus cash to the value.*

The resulting difference in net value to the owners was only $100,000!

In essence, the owners would have taken on tremendous debt and substantially increased their risk, for an increase in the projected net to the owners of just $100,000.

I'LL BE WEALTHY WHEN I SELL MY BUSINESS
LESSON TWO

A stable, privately held business, even a relatively small one, has the ability to provide a very nice lifestyle for its owners. This is accomplished in two ways: salary and distribution of profits.

Salary

Most business owners tend to pay themselves more for the work they do than they would pay an employee for doing the same work. If the owner could hire a manager for $100,000 to perform the management tasks required, he may well decide to pay himself $150,000 to do the same job. The difference is usually termed surplus compensation.—in this case $50,000.

Distribution of Profits

In addition, the owners may also be able to take advantage of some of the business profits after what they pay themselves as "salary." Say the same owner who is paying himself $150,000 a year has a profitable business with sales of $5 million, and that earns a net income of $250,000. If the company is mature, it may not need all of that net income to fund the ongoing business. So the owner may choose to pay some of that profit out to himself. Perhaps he takes $100,000 of that $250,000 net income and pays it out to himself. In total, Mr. Business Owner would be personally grossing $250,000 a year from his business.

What Is the Business Worth?

Now let's say that Mr. Business Owner decides that, despite the nice living he's making from his profitable business, he's tired and doesn't want to deal with the business anymore. So he decides to sell it. What kind of lifestyle will he be able to support with the proceeds from selling the business? Table 1 shows how the players in the deal business, the business of buying and selling businesses, are going to look at his company and derive a value for it.

TABLE 1

Calculation of Cash Flow:

Income before taxes $250,000
     Plus:
     Surplus Owner's Compensation .... <u>50,000</u>

Adjusted Income before taxes $300,000
     Plus:
     Depreciation.. <u>200,000</u>

Cash Flow or IBITDA $500,000

    A buyer is going to give Mr. Business Owner credit for the difference between the amount he pays himself for work and the $100,000 the buyer would pay an employee for the same job, and add back the surplus compensation. That will give us an adjusted net income for the business of $300,000. In addition, there are other things that a buyer will give the owner credit for, because they do not reflect the underlying operation and cash flow of the business.
    The other items that the owner commonly receives credit for,

and are added back to income, are the non-cash expenses and the cost of borrowed capital, interest (remember that the borrowed capital—debt—is going to be subtracted from the gross proceeds).

The non-cash expenses usually show up in a company's financial statements as depreciation and amortization. The cost of borrowed capital shows up as interest.

Let's assume in the case we're discussing, that we have $200,000 of depreciation cost. Since it is a fairly mature business and it is not reinvesting much, the buyer will give us credit for all of the non-cash charges. Now we have cash flow (IBITDA) of $500,000.

What will a buyer pay for that much cash flow? Well, as we'll discover later, the standard average multiplier of cash flow in valuing businesses is 4 to 4.5. So 4 times $500,000 is $2 million. A multiple of 4.5 yields $2.25 million. Let's give our owner the benefit of the doubt and say he gets a splendid price for his business equal to 5 times cash flow, a significant premium over average multiples. That would give our business owner $2.5 million.

Will I Be Wealthy?

It sounds like a lot of money: $2.5 million. But there are some things our owner is going to have to account for. Of course, he has to pay taxes. If taxes are 20 percent, he will be left with $2 million. If he has no other investments, this is what our business owner will have available to support his lifestyle from now on. A prudent financial manager may tell this business owner that an earnings rate of 5 percent on his nest egg is a conservative and safe number. At 5 percent this owner will earn $100,000 per year.

So this business owner has gone from a $250,000 income to a $100,000 income *even though we sold his business at a significant premium...which is very optimistic and probably not realistic in the first place.*

> *Myth: If you transform the market value of your business into a financial investment asset, that will adequately cover your financial security needs.*

Reality: If you transform the market value of your business into a financial investment asset, it most likely will "not" cover the same level of income you have enjoyed as a business owner.

PRIMING THE PUMP
LESSON THREE

In the United States today, there is a general lack of understanding as to what creates wealth from the ownership of a business. This is due primarily to the fact that most individuals who are advisors in this area—lawyers, accountants, personal financial planners, asset managers—do not understand the *entirety* of the process of successfully creating wealth from a privately held business.

These important advisors are typically compartmentalized into their particular areas of specialization. For example, an accountant gets involved with the tax aspects, the attorney gets involved in the legal aspects, and the asset manager takes the money and invests it. The business owner exacerbates the problem, because he treats his advisors as individuals rather than members of a team. *In fact, the business owner often goes out of his way to keep the advisors separate, as if they were competitors.* As a result, the owner doesn't get the advantage of combining the different points of view into a coherent plan for success.

> *In the United States today, there is a general lack of understanding as to what creates wealth from the ownership of a business.*

So, which of these individuals understands the entirety of the process? *That's* an issue. Your average business owner just sort of bumbles along until he comes to a painful juncture, when he's suddenly confronted with the reality—he needs an integrated team working for him with a comprehensive, integrated plan.

Myth: As a business owner, you should trust your company's wealth creation strategies to either a single advisor—or trust your own intuition.

> **Reality:** *There are lots of details that can kill the quality of your eventual payout. You need all the experienced help you can get!*

In my experience, 60 to 70 percent of business owners do not have a business plan. And of those who do, most of their plans have serious flaws. I would say that most business plans project wildly overoptimistic numbers, and they miss some of the major, very important points—most notably, they don't include a *return on investment process* or *calculation* for the owner. Realistically projecting key aspects of the business in an integrated plan is crucial for any rational understanding of how the business activity will turn into *real wealth* that will provide for the owner's future independence.

What are the component pieces of a wealth creation plan? Does your plan have *realistic* sales and marketing assumptions and execution tools? Do you understand the critical variables that affect operational and financial performance? Do you have methods in place to measure these variables and use them to get the results you want from your business?

And if you do all that, do you know how to take the money out of your business in a disciplined way that doesn't endanger the business? Will you spend this money, or save it to create future wealth? How do you take it out in a tax-advantageous manner? Most importantly, do you really believe that this list of basically straightforward business tools is something you will master by yourself with no assistance?

YOUR *SHORTCUTS TO SECURITY:*

- Thousands of people start businesses with the expectation that they will earn a comfortable retirement, if not at least a wealthy lifestyle, from that business… *most of them will end up being disappointed.*
- A great many of these disappointing results are unnecessary. They evolve from lack of knowledge, and misconceptions.
- Mistaking growth for the be all and end all, misunderstanding the cash flow cycle, and expecting a business sale to automatically create wealth are just a few of these misconceptions.
- Do you have a realistic business and wealth creation plan?

CHAPTER TWO

The Journey to Ownership Consulting

When I began writing this book, I grappled with the idea of including a complete personal and professional background. My conclusion, ultimately, was based on this precept: If I am to have any credibility imparting this information, my readers must understand that I have indeed learned from my mistakes. In other words, none of this is theory. Unfortunately.

So, here goes. I was born in Brooklyn, New York, and raised in Connecticut. I received degrees in political science and French at the University of Connecticut. I spent two years with Uncle Sam in the U.S. Army, after which I went on to the Georgetown School of Foreign Service. I discovered that my couple of years in the Army had changed me quite substantially and that I looked at government service as just the military without a uniform.

At the conclusion of my service—by this time I was twenty-six years old—I decided that I needed to go into business. However, I also needed to eat. I took a job in the commercial banking industry, starting at the very bottom as a branch banker. Fortunately, I was in a bank that believed in cross training and delegation, and I was promoted into a commercial lending position.

For my next job, I convinced a bank in Maryland that I really was a commercial lender. These were the days in the seventies when we didn't even have statewide banking, let alone a national bank. It was a Baltimore-based bank, and I was in charge of calling on the Washington, DC, area. Shortly after I arrived, my boss handed me a leveraged buyout loan to negotiate and close. From then on, I was drawn to the area of buyouts and acquisitions. I had done a $3 million loan for that deal, which probably would be the equivalent of $15 million in today's dollars. I loved the acquisitions field. I studied it daily and met a lot of people, predominantly local people in the business.

> We became a legitimate national phenomenon, and I was on top of the world. Then...I learned the hard way how not to deal in a bureaucratic environment under stress and managed to get myself and my entire department fired.

In banking, your toughest task is getting in front of people and differentiating yourself from the rest of the market. It doesn't matter if you are a national, international, or corporate calling officer. I had once met someone outside of my industry that operated a listing service for acquirers and sellers—so I introduced the concept to my bank as a method to differentiate my services.

I was a huge success, or, I should say, my *listing service* was a success. By 1979 I had three hundred subscribers to that service, listing brokers and companies for sale, which we linked up with potential buyers. In 1979, *Inc.* magazine wrote an article about us. After that, we added another 1,500 subscribers to our database, literally in sixty days. We were very much on the cutting edge in the development of the concept of the leveraged buyout, and we became a specialized acquisition financing group.

We became a legitimate national phenomenon, and I was on top of the world. People on Wall Street were calling us. People who were in the leveraged buyout business called us. My boss ended up in New York. Things couldn't have been any better. But from that pinnacle there was nowhere else to go but down.

With impeccable timing, in 1980 there was a tremendous financial crisis. Interest rates went through the roof, prime went up to more than 20 percent...everyone was in a panic. As for me, I learned the hard way how *not* to deal in a bureaucratic environment under stress and managed to get myself and my entire department fired.

At the time, I had three kids under the age of five. I was given three weeks severance pay. If I had $3,000 in the bank, that was the extent of my resources. I was also in major debt. My wife and I had a home mortgage, and she was not working. We had some credit cards. If there was one bright spot in the world, it would be that we didn't have much of a car loan.

So I went from being an employee to being an instant entrepreneur. To this day, I can't remember exactly what I did to convince people to hire me in those years, at least that first year. But I managed to find a few people who would give me some money for my business advice. That was the start of my entrepreneurial career. There was someone who wanted to get into the publication business, for example. He wanted to replicate what we had done at the bank, so I did some consulting work for him. What I really wanted to do, though, were buyout and acquisition deals.

> *When I left the business in 1993, my transactions totaled more than half a billion dollars.*

I knew some people who were putting together a new investment banking firm, and they brought me on as a sort of junior member. That was in 1981. I literally started at the bottom. I was the guy who wrote up all the reports and did all the research and grunt work, and they gradually taught me the deal side of the business. As time went on, I started doing more and more of the actual deal work within the company. Over the twelve-year period that I was there, I went from being the junior-most person, to being a 50 percent owner and managing partner.

I did a tremendous number of transactions. When I left the business in 1993, my transactions totaled more than half a billion dollars. We had also endured just about every ownership mistake known to man.

The original two partners who had put the business together got into a huge conflict, one accusing the other of embezzlement, the other tossing accusations of nepotism. The break-up was ugly. That's when I became a 50 percent owner with the individual I ended up staying with. I learned some valuable lessons along the road about taking things at face value, not doing due diligence, and not listening to both sides of a story.

Unfortunately, the attorney of the partner I stayed with gave us some terrible advice in terms of not doing anything to develop any new business. Due to the drama, we were essentially on the sidelines for a year during one of the best acquisition markets that had been had for some time.

In effect, we had to start all over again. We had to literally create new momentum. But just as we were getting our momentum going, we were hit by Black Monday in 1987. For all intents and purposes, we had half a million dollars in fees disappear that day that had been dependent on junk bond financing.

We tried to get back to the point where we had once been by putting together our own funds to invest into companies. Then we took a couple of hits. First, the only time we truly took equity in a deal, it turned out badly; after having put many transactions together that had been very successful for both sides, our own equity deal cratered. And then I had another client who stiffed us on our fee. *And...* in the meantime, my partner, who had been our primary new business development person, was not doing so well and I didn't know why. I later found out that he had developed terminal cancer and hadn't told me.

The bottom line is this: I went through a process of continuing to fund a difficult business, putting lots of money into it, and trying to keep it going.

At the same time, I had gone through some profound personal changes. When I was young, doing deals was a very ego-satisfying thing—*big dollars, wheeling and dealing, etc.* The more that I worked and matured, however, the more that the deal-making was less important to me than the fulfillment of doing a good job for my clients.

I really liked our clients. They were good people who worked hard. I wanted to see them get the results that they deserved, but I was getting very discouraged with the nature of the investment banking business. First, it was difficult for me to accept that when we closed a successful deal and I delivered the sellers a lot of money, they weren't always ecstatically happy. In fact, the sellers were very often unsettled and unhappy to be selling their businesses. And second, no matter what I did, people tended to distrust me. That's the nature of being the intermediary, the broker.

After that, we had one particularly bad situation where a my partner's good friend had brought us on board for a deal, and I knew I had done a phenomenal transaction for him. Yet at the successful conclusion of the transaction, the friend actually accused us of selling him down the river. Despite getting him a premium price for his business, he was unhappy with the abrupt transition in his life. I could hardly believe that my successful effort for him had resulted in his unhappiness.

My love of the business had waned, which had a definitive effect on my ability to close deals and find new ones. The combination of that and my partner's illness caused us to spiral downhill.

When neither of us would acknowledge our problems, we lost everything we had worked toward. This is sort of a classic entrepreneurial problem when things start going bad.

There's a tendency to say, "Well, you know, let's just dig in our heels and work harder." Even though you're not recognizing that there's been a real change, a fundamental change has indeed taken place.

> *We had gotten to a point where I had pretty much leveraged everything that I owned. There was nothing left but my debt.*

We had gotten to a point where I had pretty much leveraged everything that I owned. Cumulatively, I incurred personal debt in credit cards and second mortgage loans in the low six figures. I could no longer meet payroll, because there was no further credit available to me. I was tapped out. There was nothing left but my debt.

Around that time I found out from my partner's son-in-law what my partner's situation was in terms of his illness. It was then that I finally realized why my partner had not consummated the commitments for the investment fund we had been raising, which had been meant to be our savior. Specifically, he wasn't going to put his friends' money—and he was the one with all the money contacts—into a transaction when he thought he was going to die. I realized at that point that the partnership was dead. I knew I had to make a choice in terms of what I was going to do for the good of my family.

I could have taken our company into a larger investment banking firm—we had a pretty valuable direct marketing mechanism with ten years' worth of data substantiation— but that would have meant throwing my partner to the wolves, which I wasn't going to do. He had a great number of personal issues, and I was just not willing to contribute to making life worse for him, especially since I no longer wanted to be in the deal business anyway. My wife and I then decided we wanted to move to New Mexico for a fresh start. Long before, we had said if we were ever going to start all over again, we would start where we really wanted to live. So, I picked up and went to Albuquerque, literally driving there with my clothes and my computer, got a week-by-week rental, and started to answer job ads. At that point, I was technically bankrupt, though I did not actually declare bankruptcy.

> *I wasn't performing the typical business consulting script. I found I was drawn to asking: What do you want from your business?*

Within three weeks, I was fortunate enough to get a job. I had made a vow at that point that I was never going to be an entrepreneur again, and I would never do any more deals.

I was out of the deal business *for good*. My new job was sufficient enough to fund my purchase of a new home— the one thing I did still have was equity in my previous home, so we were able to transfer that over.

So, I brought my wife and the kids to New Mexico and started what was supposed to be a new, non-entrepreneurial life. Well, that lasted about thirteen months. *Thirteen months.* That's all the time it took for me to realize that I was no longer employee material.

When you've been on your own for so long and you've called your own shots, playing the employee game is very difficult to return to. That was true for me, and it was that attitude that got me fired again. But this time I saw it coming, and I had already organized my exit and converted three of my suppliers into clients.

New Mexico was unusual at the time in that a lot of things that were somewhat well-known in other parts of the country in terms of technical and related expertise were not known there. It was certainly a market of opportunity for advisors with experience. Through my involvement with soccer, I had a very good networking capability, and I was able to get involved with the community and get people to know and see what I was doing.

For the next couple of years I consulted on an ad hoc basis. About two years after starting, I made a very important discovery. I discovered that I was not consulting with people about their businesses in the traditional sense. I wasn't performing the typical business consulting script. I wasn't telling the business owner what kind of market share he should have, or "you need to be more efficient," or "the business needs to grow."

I found I was drawn to asking and understanding the business owner's responses to a very incisive question: *What do you want from your business?*

This is the critical factor about The Podolny Method©. It revolves around the premise to this very simple question, and understanding the implications of the responses to that question.

It was 1995 when I had this epiphany, yet I didn't know how to communicate it, especially when owners and advisors expected the typical old business consulting script.

I spent another couple of years saying to myself, *Okay, how do I communicate this? How do I put this into a form where I can explain it?* Because it's not that easy. I spent a lot of time and money trying to figure out how to communicate the specifics of my approach for consulting with business owners.

> *The methods are time-tested and successful for all types of businesses and for every type of business owner. This people-centric path to business success, personal fulfillment, and security continues to work for me and for our clients... it will for you too.*

And then...I had a situation with a client in California who wanted me to do some consulting work, and I realized that I had to get myself organized if I wanted him to be able to complete a particular project in an economical manner. And that's when I realized that I, in fact, did have a methodology that I could put into a concise format others could understand. That realization led to the writing of my first book, *Make Your Business Serve You.*

After writing that book, I continued working with hundreds of different entrepreneurial businesses. Among them were very successful businesses that had gotten to a certain point of success but didn't know how to go to the next level, because they'd never been there before. There were people who had good businesses and were asking, "How do I get out of this thing? How do I cash in?" And then there were those who had significant structural problems and the bank was knocking at the door ready to liquidate their assets.

The crucial essence of The Podolny Method© is asking owners about themselves first—what they want, who they are, what makes them tick—and then looking at the business in light of their answers. Using The Podolny Method© changes the whole equation for consulting with business owners.

We call it "ownership consulting" because we don't look solely at the business processes; we are owner-centric, concentrating on the human element of how privately held businesses succeed and provide success to their owners. Most important, we ensure that each owner's personal, individual definition of success is the guiding force in our work. Understanding the owner from a human perspective entirely transforms what we are evaluating in terms of the business and how we set and accomplish goals.

I had some help from a supportive family in terms of the financial side of incubating The Podolny Group in the early years, but in my psychological rebirthing and in learning life lessons, I was pretty much on my own. What a journey it has been.

So, you see, my methods are not simply theory. They never have been. The methods are time-tested and successful for all types of businesses and for every type of business owner. This people-centric path to business success, personal fulfillment, and security continues to work for me and for our clients... and it will for you too.

YOUR *SHORTCUTS TO SECURITY:*

- The precepts of this book are based on tangible personal experience, both in my own life and in the lives of my clients.
- I built up an innovative, groundbreaking investment banking service in a commercial bank, but managed to get my department and myself fired.
- I built a mergers/acquisitions business that closed more than a half a billion dollars in transactions only to see it fail, leaving me to stare bankruptcy in the face.
- Ultimately, I found success and peace-of-mind focusing on providing consulting that answered this simple question:

What do you, as a person, really want from the life of your business ownership?

CHAPTER THREE

The MBA Fallacy

Over the last thirty years I have had the opportunity to work with thousands of business owners, covering the broad spectrum of American business. I have worked with pure startups, as well as companies doing hundreds of millions in sales. I have had clients who were in software development, apparel retailing, agricultural distribution, food service, transportation, and on and on. I have had clients in Maine and in San Diego, in Seattle and in Miami. I have worked with owners from New York City and from Cedar Rapids, Iowa.

> *What I have been most impressed with is the universality of the condition of these business owners. The vast majority of them are discontented.*

What I have been most impressed with is the universality of the condition of these business owners. The vast majority of them are discontented. They are dissatisfied with the end results of their years of effort and risk. And this is not just a function of their material situations. Some of the unhappiest business owners I have met have been those who others, on the outside, would say are the most successful!

Why is this? Why is it that the endeavor of business ownership, that requires such commitment, so frequently leads to personal dissatisfaction? A great many of the people who come to me for my expertise have a fair amount of psychological pain and agony over their business issues, whatever they are.

> *Even when business owners go into a venture with some planning, they rarely factor their personal goals and objectives into the equation independently from their business goals and objectives.*

This is especially true regarding dealings with a business partner or when the owner feels like he has been working awfully hard for a very long time and still doesn't feel any closer to reaching the goals that are most personally important.

Let's look at an analogy to understand the nature inherent to the problem that most business owners face in their attempts to build a business that will provide for their own personal success and fulfillment. Imagine that a person wants to build a house. He makes the decision that he is going to build this house himself. The next thing he does is buy what he thinks he will need to build the house. He purchases a piece of land, some lumber, plumbing supplies, concrete, electrical supplies, furniture, and appliances. He goes to his land, and he starts to work. He brings in subcontractors and has them start working.

Each day he has to make myriad decisions. Where should he store the things he bought? Who should be working and when? All the while, he is thinking, *I wonder what this house will look like when it is done?* Doesn't sound like the recipe for a very successful building project, does it?

The more logical method would have been for him to seriously think about what he wants from the house before he ever starts the process of building. Does he want to be close to others, or does he want privacy and distance? Does he want a lot of space and many rooms, or does he want something smaller and more manageable? What architectural style does he want? How much is he willing to spend?

With these decisions made, he might go to an architect and have a design and blueprints made. He could go to a realtor and commission a search for a piece of property. If acting as his own general contractor, he could plan out a timetable for construction, negotiate subcontracting agreements, and begin the methodical process of building, always with a picture in mind of what the finished product will look like. Planning before beginning the building process would alleviate many potential problems indeed.

> *Ultimately, if you do not include the human element (i.e., you, the owner!) into the equation of analyzing and planning within your business, the chances of achieving personal fulfillment from your business activity are very low.*

Yet if you look around at all the businesses that you know, my guess is that, like me, you will find there are very few business owners who ever went through a process of evaluating themselves and their business before they started "building."

If they had determined what they were hoping to achieve and had put a plan in place to make it happen, they would have had a much better chance of building a business that could truly serve their needs.

I cannot tell you the number of times I have asked a business owner about the history of his company, and he responded, "Well, I saw an opportunity in [insert any industry or business segment], got started, and here I am." In other words, he had a feeling there was an opportunity, and he started to operate, without a vision or a plan, just like our imaginary homebuilder above. The difficulties that these business owners face are no less unsettling than the unfortunate homebuilder who didn't plan before starting to build.

Even when business owners go into a venture with some planning, they rarely factor their personal goals and objectives into the equation independently from their business goals and objectives. And it's not just the owner who fails to make these considerations. It is true of almost all of their advisors and everywhere they look for information. Even when business planning is conducted and advice is sought, seldom do the owner's personal considerations come into the process. I call this the *MBA Fallacy*, because rarely in formal business education programs (of which the MBA is the most prominent) is the owner asked, "What do you want?" The emphasis is always on the business itself, not on the owner. "The business needs to grow."—"The business needs this; the business needs that."

Ultimately, if you do not include the human element (i.e., you, the owner!) into the equation of analyzing and planning within your business, the chances of achieving personal fulfillment from your business activity are very low.

YOUR *SHORTCUTS TO SECURITY:*

- Despite outside appearances, an amazingly high number of business owners are discontented with their lives.
- Can you imagine building a house with no drawings and no plans? Yet this is the way many in business start and continue to run their companies.
- Even if there is a formal business plan,. a plan that does not include the human element of the owner is unlikely to bring personal fulfillment.

PART TWO

Before the Shortcut— an Honest Evaluation

CHAPTER FOUR

Who Are You?
What Do You Want?
Establishing Your Personal Goals First

How ironic it is that we humans take so little time to think about what makes us happy before we make decisions that lock us into years and years of a particular lifestyle. It would seem to be the most natural thing in the world. After all, isn't that one of the basic motivating factors in life—the desire to be happy?

Yet ask any random sampling of people what will make them happy and you often get formulaic answers. "Money will make me happy." Or, "Fame will make me happy." Nevertheless, even business owners who, by any objective measure, achieve wealth and recognition are often lacking in happiness. Therefore, if you are to make your business serve you, then establishing your personal goals is where we must start.

Work is a major component of almost everyone's life. We probably spend more of our time with our work than any other single activity.

That which is going to make you happy, content, and satisfied is not necessarily simple to identify. It is a combination of factors, some large and some small. I categorize these as Career, Personal Time, Personal Energy, and Values.

CAREER

Work is a major component of almost everyone's life. We probably spend more of our time with our work than any other single activity. If we were not business owners, we would have a career or a job doing something else. People who like their work tend to be happier and healthier, in general, than those who do not. Therefore, in The Podolny Method© we ask that the business owner assume that they are not the owner, but an employee, and look at what they like and do not like about their work. We want to know what type of work they most enjoy doing.

I am reminded of a client of mine who had a very successful distribution business. Distribution businesses tend to operate on very thin margins. This particular business owner loved to sell, but hated dealing with detail and minutiae. Nothing made him happier than getting in front of customers. He started out as a salesperson before taking the company over from his father. When he inherited the business, the first thing he did was to hire a sales manager and put himself in charge of operations because he thought that was what he had to do. As head of operations he was required to oversee purchasing, warehousing, and distribution. Was it any wonder that this person was frustrated? He had managed himself into a position where he was doing exactly what he most disliked!

PERSONAL TIME

Another major component of our personal side, is our personal time outside of work. I have found that business owners have two concerns about personal non-job related time.

One of these concerns is the adequacy of personal time, meaning the amount of time available for non-job related activities—whether that is family, recreation, or simply sleep! It is not unusual

> *It is not unusual for a business owner to spend virtually every waking moment physically at, or thinking about, his business—with practically no personal time left to himself.*

for a business owner to spend virtually every waking moment physically at, or thinking about, his business—with practically no personal time left to himself.

The other aspect to consider is freedom of choice related to the use of available personal time. Many business owners find that despite having some personal time the demands of their jobs have them locked into schedules over which they have little control.

I recall the owner of a small tree service who really enjoyed his work with trees, but was completely frustrated each spring. The nature of his business was seasonal. It required him to work seven days a week for twelve weeks during the season, even though at other times of the year he had plenty of personal time.

Originally his business had been a single-person operation. As the quality of his work became known, his business grew, and he hired more employees. His operation became more successful and serviced more customers.

Unfortunately, the season when his business was the most intense and required his constant attention was also the same time that his kids were playing sports; he really wanted to attend their games and be a part of their lives. Despite having plenty of personal time to spend with family during other times, the spring crunch did not allow him any time to spend with his family for almost three months of every year. This imbalance in the demands on his time caused him great resentment and personal dissatisfaction and caused his family great disappointment. This business owner felt imprisoned by his business.

Issues related to time usage and scheduling are among the most frequent causes of business owner dissatisfaction.

PERSONAL ENERGY

One of the defining characteristics of business owners is their energy level. Business owners, when they start out, typically work twelve to fourteen-hour days, sometimes seven days a week. And they do this out of desire and self-motivation. One of the things that has motivated me most in developing my program is my respect and admiration for this internal energy and commitment manifested by business owners. This energy, however, is not a renewable resource.

Sooner or later it begins to be depleted, and the owner will have to slow down.

For planning purposes it is critical that business owners recognize where they are on the energy curve relative to the tasks that need to be accomplished to achieve their personal goals. Allowing themselves to get into a position of having to work at the same level as when they were younger because personal financial demands require it is one of the worst traps in which business owners can find themselves.

PERSONAL VALUES

People have complex motivations. Business owners are frequently people with strong principles. While this is a good thing, a person's values can become a source of conflict.

> *Business owners are frequently people with strong principles. While this is a good thing, a person's values can become a source of conflict.*

A client of mine had built a very profitable direct marketing company. The primary product sold by this company was diet pills. This was a lucrative business that provided him and his family with a substantial lifestyle. All was fine until the owner converted to a new religion. Suddenly he found that the new values derived from his religion led him to question the ethics of the diet pill business. He was attached to the lifestyle the business had provided him, but there were very few business alternatives available to him that would offer the same return on his investment. He discovered that because of his new values he was in a position of personal conflict concerning his business.

COMPLETING A PERSONAL GOAL INVENTORY

The first step to putting your business ownership in harmony with your lifestyle is to catalog your career and personal goals. Examine each of your personal aspects, including both the person you are in your career and your personal life apart from your business.

It is very important in conducting this exercise that you set aside your concerns and considerations about your business as it exists today. Examine your personal goals, career preferences, personal time needs, personal energy issues, and personal values separately from any business concerns.

When I work with my clients, they will frequently answer questions in terms of what the business is demanding of them, because their lives currently revolve around their business. Focusing on yourself, separate from your business, is critical to the success of discovering your real personal desires. These discoveries, in turn, are important to formulating plans to transform your business into an enterprise that serves your goals and needs.

YOUR *SHORTCUTS TO SECURITY:*

- Seeking happiness and contentment seems the most logical of goals, yet few take the time to look at themselves and understand what will truly provide for those goals.
- We find in those who are business owners, a number of factors that time and again affect their personal well-being, including work preferences, outside interests, energy level, and time.

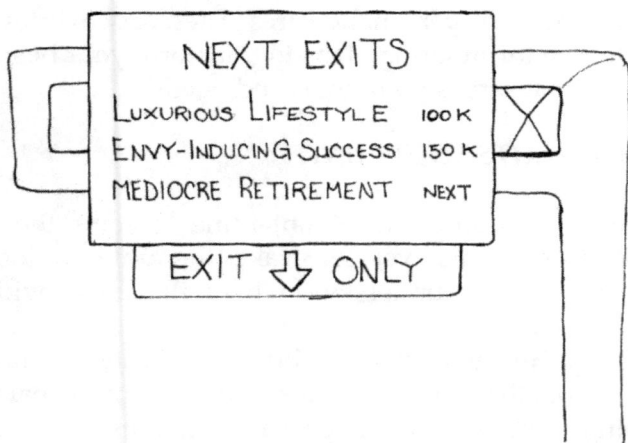

NEXT EXITS

Luxurious Lifestyle   100 K
Envy-Inducing Success   150 K
Mediocre Retirement   NEXT

EXIT ⬇ ONLY

CHAPTER FIVE

What Is the Role of Money in Your Life? Learning How to Adopt the Role of Shareholder. The Importance of an Exit Strategy. Defining Your Personal Financial Goals.

One of the most compelling myths that drives business decision-making is that the primary goal of business ownership is to become rich. The determination of who is rich and who is not rich, of course, is quite subjective. To their employees, most business owners seem rich. But to themselves, most business owners always seem to find themselves lacking. The pursuit of wealth frequently dominates the thinking of business owners, especially during the initial stages of their careers. After all, isn't that magical combination of the vision of opportunity, combined with the will and energy to pursue it, the core of entrepreneurial activity?

> *In the simplest terms, money is either the tool for achieving a lifestyle or a measure of one's achievement in the competitive game of life.*

As business owners get beyond the initial vision and into the realities of operating their businesses, there is frequently a shift in their opinions of how much is enough. It is not uncommon for business owners who have been working for decades to settle for much less than they would have years earlier, because they want to get free of the responsibilities associated with owning a business. Evaluating your personal financial goals starts with a study of what money means to you.

WHAT IS THE ROLE OF MONEY IN YOUR LIFE?

In the simplest terms, *money is either the tool for achieving a lifestyle or a measure of one's achievement in the competitive game of life.*

For a significant portion of owners, business is not just a venture for achieving a lifestyle. It is a competition. And while wealth is not the only measurement for competitive success, it is frequently the measurement of choice. If business owners feel they have not created the wealth that they initially anticipated, it is not uncommon for them to feel that they have failed.

The other use of money is for the establishment of a lifestyle. Lifestyles can be lavish or simple. The individual's choice of lifestyle has a significant influence on the implicit performance requirements of a business. The most important aspect of understanding your lifestyle requirements is to first quantify them. When a variable can be quantified it installs an empirical factor into the planning equation. This is highly desirable.

It is important to recognize that whatever your choice concerning the role of money, *it is your personal decision.* Very little is accomplished by assigning someone else's values to your situation. The key is to recognize what you *really* want and then accept it. If you try to plan based upon some set of values established by others, no matter how well intended, you are guaranteed to put yourself into a position of conflict and unhappiness.

ADOPTING YOUR ROLE AS SHAREHOLDER

One of the keys to truly getting your business to serve you, rather than you serving your business, is to understand that you, the owner, have taken on many different roles as they relate to your business. It is the balancing and reconciliation of these different, often conflicting, roles that provide the basic analytical process necessary for achieving a business plan that will get your business to serve you.

One of the most important and ignored roles that the business owner should recognize is that of shareholder. This role is much different from that of being the manager of the business. The manager is concerned with all aspects of business performance and operation. The shareholder is an investor. The investor's primary concerns are: *How well is the investment performing?* and *Is the investment meeting my portfolio requirements?*

> *One of the most important and ignored roles that the business owner should recognize is that of shareholder. The shareholder is an investor. The investor's primary concern is: How well is the investment performing?*

Portfolio requirements? That's a strange-sounding term for a person who only owns one business. Let's look at this more closely.

Imagine for a moment that you have no role whatsoever in the running of your business. It is strictly an investment that you made with your money. But it is an investment that happens to dominate your personal balance sheet. It probably represents the single largest asset that you own. Now if you are strictly an investor, what would you expect of this asset? Typically, investors look at criteria such as:

- **Performance** - How this company is doing compared to others in its industry.
- **Risk** - What the chances are that the asset could be lost or diminished.
- **Yield** - How much the asset can spin-off in current return (above and beyond any salary paid to a manager; remember you are thinking as an investor, not a manager).
- **Potential for Gain** - What kind of long-term increase in the value of the asset can be achieved.

If you looked at your business in this light, would it represent a good investment? Would you, in your role as shareholder, hold onto this investment or could you get better performance from the investment by liquidating it and redeploying the funds into a diversified portfolio? Every business should be evaluated in the light of the dispassionate shareholder in order to give another, empirical point of measure in the personal planning process.

EXIT PLANNING—UNDERSTANDING YOUR FUTURE FINANCIAL REQUIREMENTS

Business ownership is not forever, though like teenagers many business owners behave as if they will be going on in the same mode forever. Business ownership is like every other aspect of life; it has a beginning, a growth period, a period of maturity, a decline, and an end.

Yet the end of one's personal life rarely coincides with the end of business ownership. For the vast majority of business owners, the exit from a business represents a major life change from one role to another. Yet few business owners even think about an exit strategy, let alone give it prominence in planning and decision-making. If you perceive your life as a business owner to be a story, the quality of your exit will determine if that story has a happy or a sad ending. Planning for an eventual exit from your business is crucial for enhancing the chances of a happy ending to the story.

There are three things that must be established to begin working on an exit strategy. These are:

- What is the time horizon for when you wish to exit your business?
- How much will you need to have accumulated in personal wealth before exiting the business in order to maintain your desired lifestyle?
- What is a realistic valuation formula for your business, and how marketable is it, really?

Having an idea of when you want to exit and how much you need to have accumulated by that time provides you with a specific target in terms of personal wealth creation. Having a realistic plan for achieving that target is critical.

There are only two ways that I have observed for a business owner to create wealth. The first is to keep the business as lean as possible, limiting overhead growth, and adopting a program of taking profits out of the business and investing those funds in financial instruments in order to create personal wealth. The second is to build a business that is truly attractive as an acquisition and create your personal wealth via the sale of that business. Going public is a variation of that path.

Most business owners have unrealistically optimistic ideas concerning the sale value of their business. The factors affecting the value of a business and its marketability are myriad and complex.

A frequent mistake owners make that impacts value is growing their business just enough to require using up all the surplus capital to cover increasing overhead expenses, but not enough to produce demonstrable profit growth. If the growth of your business does not produce profit growth, you may be building a trap for yourself, whereby the surplus capital that could go to you is used up, meaning that the value of your business is not growing.

> *Most business owners have unrealistically optimistic ideas concerning the sale value of their business.*

COMPLETING A PERSONAL
FINANCIAL GOALS INVENTORY

The next step in the process is cataloging your personal financial goals. Go through each section of this chapter. Pay particular attention to the discipline of being a shareholder and to the quantification of your exit requirements (Use the Financial Independence Requirements Spreadsheet found in Appendix C to assist you). As noted in the previous chapter, put aside your concerns and considerations about the business as it exists at this moment. Look only at your personal considerations for now.

YOUR *SHORTCUTS TO SECURITY:*

- What is the role of money in your life?
- Is money a tool to provide a lifestyle? Or is it a measure of your success? Or both?
- To get a real payoff from your business ownership, you need to look at your business as if it were an outside investment—as if you were not involved.
- This needs to be balanced against the financial requirements of your life after your business ownership is complete—your exit plan.

CHAPTER SIX

Evaluating Your Business. Developing a Complete and Accurate Picture of What Your Business Is Now.

Getting business owners to focus on their personal requirements often requires a major shift in perception. This is because most owners assume that their personal life is synonymous with their business life. In the preceding chapters we have focused primarily on the reasons that this is not true. We have provided the initial tools for helping owners evaluate and categorize their personal goals and objectives separate from their business requirements.

However, the owner is still in command of a business. That business is the owner's source of income and lifestyle. It represents a huge investment of the owner's time and money. Finally, the business has a role and position within society that is totally separate from the person who owns it. If that business were to suddenly cease operating, many would be affected. Some would be out of work. Others who used its products or services would have to find another source. Suppliers would have to find another customer.

A business is the owner's source of income and lifestyle. It represents a huge investment of the owner's time and money.

A business is an entity in an environment where it is in constant competition. It must compete effectively if it is to serve all of its constituents' interests, especially its owner's. Therefore, just as we have looked at our various personal requirements and roles independent of the business, we now need to look at the requirements and roles of the business independent of the owner.

The Podolny Method© conducts the process of defining a business in three steps:

- The first of these is a simple cataloging of what the business is now. This means listing all aspects of the business, from its products and customers to its facilities and assets to its means of control and management.
- The second step requires making value judgments concerning the relative strengths and weaknesses of the individual aspects of the business as defined in the first step.
- The last step involves the definition of changes that need to take place in the future if the business is to be competitive, given the information generated in the first two steps. This chapter will assist you in the first two steps of this process. The next chapter will cover the third step.

CATALOGING YOUR BUSINESS OPERATIONS

We start this process with a complete description of what your business is now. I have found that many business people have a far more difficult time with this than usually would be expected. It is one of the tendencies of business owners to become overly focused on their own daily activities at the expense of understanding the larger picture within which they must compete.

I suggest that you seek the aid of an objective third party to help you develop this description. You should cover the main areas of your business, including:

- its product or service lines
- the market that it serves
- its sources of supply
- how it sells

- how it delivers its product
- how it functions (such as how distribution or R&D are handled)
- the physical plant
- personnel and management
- its competition and how it stacks up competitively
- industry trends
- its internal systems and controls
- its financial history

EVALUATING THE CURRENT STATUS OF YOUR BUSINESS

Now that you have a catalog of your business operations, you can begin the process of evaluating it. In its simplest terms, this evaluation focuses on two things—what are the strengths and weaknesses of the business?

Go back to the description of your business you have just finished. Go through each of the sections and make a value judgment. Is this an area that you consider a strength of your business? Is it an area that you are confident is carrying its weight? Are you free to concentrate on other parts of your business because of its good performance, or is it an area that you consider weak? Is it a cause of ongoing problem-solving, and is this area taking substantial amounts of management time? After going through each segment of your business and making this evaluation as to whether it is an area of strength or weakness, compile your results.

The critical part of this step is the determination of why a particular operational area is strong or weak. As in previous steps of The Podolny Method©, honest and accurate appraisal is critical to your success in putting together a plan of action that will truly serve you.

In all steps of The Podolny Method©, it is more important to do things right than to do things quickly. Distance and dispassion from daily business management is important. I suggest that you set a time for working on this step that is totally free and clear of other business responsibilities. For example, weekends away from the business make this activity go more smoothly.

YOUR *SHORTCUTS TO SECURITY:*

- Your business is your major asset.
- Even when focusing on a personal goal-oriented plan, remember that an effectively run business is key to that plan's success.
- It is critical to take an objective and realistic review of the business, paying attention to all the critical functions.
- With that information, strengths and weaknesses can be identified, as well as the reasons why they are strengths and weaknesses.

CHAPTER SEVEN

Defining the Goals of Your Business. What Does Your Business Need to Do to Be a Viable Competitor?

The analyses in the prior chapter are the purview of traditional business consulting. In Chapter Three, I decried the *MBA Fallacy*, which I defined as attempting to treat the ills of a business without taking into account the needs of the person, the business owner. Yet it would be equally erroneous to focus only on the owner without taking into account the needs of the business.

> *The present and future health of your business is critical, because it is the ongoing source of your present lifestyle and one of the primary tools for achieving your future goals.*

It is highly unlikely that any of the goals that come out of this process are going to be accomplished overnight. Therefore, maintaining the present and future health of your business is critical, because it is the ongoing source of your present lifestyle and one of the primary tools for achieving your future goals.

Having completed the two steps covered in the previous chapter, we now have a list of the strengths and weaknesses of your business. Taking this information, we want to go one step further. We want to specifically define the goals that we will need to achieve if the business is to be a viable competitor.

This task requires judgments on your part. You have already gone through the process of determining the strengths and weaknesses of the business and the reasons that they exist. There are three sets of judgments that need to be executed:

- First, classify each area in terms of its importance to future operating performance. The current operational strength of your business may not necessarily be the strength required to compete in the future.
- Second, determine what should be done to either maintain or build on the existing strengths or to turn around the weaknesses that have been classified as important to the future competitiveness of your business. This analysis helps in defining your business goals.
- Finally, determine what actions and resources will be required in order to execute those goals, once they are determined. These are goals and targets for change.

Let's look at each of these three sets of judgments in more detail in the following sections:

CLASSIFYING OPERATING AREAS IN TERMS OF IMPORTANCE TO FUTURE PERFORMANCE

Earlier on you were asked to determine if an operating area of your business was a strength or a weakness. Now we want you to determine just how important that operating area is, not just to your current situation, but also to your projected requirements for the future. Start with the assumption that you are working in an environment of limited resources. You do not have enough resources to do everything you want. Therefore, you must determine which operating areas are the most critical to your future competitiveness.

Here is an example. My client owned a manufacturing company. Our analysis of operations led us to identify some specific strengths and weaknesses. One of the strengths of the business was the quality of its manufacturing and its effective use of fixed assets. These strengths provided the business with substantial room for growth without additional investment. Its weaknesses were relatively poor financial and management controls, insufficient information systems, and an undeveloped sales program.

Sometimes an operating area can simultaneously be both a strength and a weakness. In this case, the business had a very lean management staff. That was a strength, because overhead was low, creating a high return on overhead load. However, that same leanness limited management time available to take on other tasks and created unnecessary risk should one of the managers ever become unavailable to work.

In classifying the importance of these strengths and weaknesses, we determined that improving sales was less important than strengthening financial and management controls. Why? The business was already operating at a profit with strong cash flow. Its manufacturing quality was strong enough that, at least in the short-term, it was getting enough business to maintain sales and cash flow.

But the thinness of management was a substantial risk factor in being able to maintain future performance. Additionally there were signs of energy burnout in the owner/managers. By improving financial and operational controls, management would be able to substantially reduce the time required to accomplish many necessary tasks and get tools that would allow the owners to improve profitability even more. Since management depth was so critical to the future success of the business, improving financial and management controls was more important than increasing sales.

AN EXERCISE FOR DEFINING GOALS AND TARGETS

You should take the information that you have already compiled, which analyzes the strengths and weaknesses of your business and now analyze each area for the actions necessary to either maintain an area of strength or to turn around an area of weakness. This is the backbone for defining the goals of your business. Be as specific as possible. Do you need to add personnel? Remove existing personnel? Add equipment? Improve the performance of a group? In some cases you will find, particularly with areas of strength, that it is not necessary to do anything.

Go through the resulting list of required actions. Consider exactly what will be required in terms of resources in order to carry out the actions necessary to maintain or turn around an area. Make sure that you take into account resources required such as time and expertise, as well as capital.

Again, be as specific as possible. These items become your primary and secondary targets.

YOUR *SHORTCUTS TO SECURITY:*

- To plan for your business and how it is going to serve your personal goals, you as an owner must understand how to evaluate and deal with its strengths and weaknesses.
- Strengths and weaknesses must be judged in relation to the future needs of the business.
- In that light, a determination should be made as to what must be done to either leverage a strength or offset a weakness.
- With this information you can begin to develop specific goals and targets for change.

CHAPTER EIGHT

Identifying and Reconciling
Conflicts between Goals

We have now completed the analytical portion of the process. From here we move into the area of problem solving—tackling the specific areas of conflict that may be keeping you from achieving the fullest rewards of business ownership. The operative phrase for achieving results at this stage is "look for the obvious."

It is possible to spend many hours looking for answers when, in fact, they are right in front of you. Unfortunately, the nature of running a business frequently calls for owners to focus on seemingly unending streams of detail. When this is the case, finding the obvious can be a challenge.

To develop a sense of dispassion, or distancing of oneself from the day-to-day, it is helpful to understand that there are only a few basic types of conflicts. Most of the struggles will fall primarily in the areas of the use of financial resources, the use of time resources, and differing goals for end results. Examples will be helpful in gaining a deeper understanding of the process of identifying and reconciling these conflicts.

EXAMPLE 1—CONFLICT IN THE USE
OF FINANCIAL RESOURCES

Let us assume that in your personal financial goal-setting you have determined a need for greater personal liquidity (meaning you wish less of your personal net worth to be at risk in the business).

But after having gone through the evaluation of your business, you have discovered that to hold on to market share and remain competitive you must grow at a fairly rapid rate.

Gaining personal liquidity will require that you take capital out of the business and redeploy it in other personal investments. Yet a business that is growing at a fairly rapid rate requires capital, meaning there is a basic conflict between these two goals. One goal requires taking capital from the business. The other calls for capital to be retained in the business.

EXAMPLE 2—CONFLICT IN THE USE
OF TIME RESOURCES

Assume that your personal non-business goal-setting has identified the desire to spend more time with your children before they grow up and leave home.

Assume that your personal career goal-setting has identified a desire to be recognized within your industry for the ideas and concepts you have promoted in your business.

Further, the analysis of your business has identified a number of areas of weakness that are going to require additional owner involvement if the business is to achieve its full potential.

Here again is a clear and basic conflict. One goal, personal non-business time use, demands that you spend less time at work. Two other goals, personal career and business requirements, demand that you spend more time at work.

EXAMPLE 3—CONFLICT BETWEEN
DESIRED END RESULTS

Assume that there are two operating shareholders in a business. One shareholder is in his sixties and the other is in his forties. The older shareholder connects his sense of self-worth and self-definition to his role as a professional. He is the classic die with his boots on. type. The younger shareholder is motivated to make a substantial amount of money and "retire early."

These two differing sets of end goals represent a built-in conflict. The goals of the younger shareholder are best served by managing the business toward a rapid building of shareholder value and planning a relatively early exit. The older shareholder is most likely to never want to exit at all.

Exit would mean a cessation of work, and that, in turn, would be a major blow to his sense of self.

IDENTIFYING CONFLICTS

Now it is time to identify all the conflicts that exist between your various goals. Make a list of the goals you identified in the previous chapters for each of your major roles: goals for personal non-work time, personal career goals, personal financial goals, and goals for business health and competitiveness.

Next, categorize all of these goals by the three main areas of potential conflict: use of time, use of capital, and end result. Some of the goals may need to be listed in more than one of the three areas of conflict. Once the goals are categorized, study each category, looking for obvious conflicts. Identify and list all of your specific goals that are in conflict.

RECONCILING CONFLICTS BETWEEN GOALS

Recognizing that there are clear conflicts is only half the battle. The other half is reconciling these conflicts so that you can work on a resolution. One characteristic of business owners that causes them much stress is their desire to find perfect solutions to these conflicts. Such solutions are rarely attainable. A significant percentage of the time there is no perfect solution—only tradeoffs. The sooner you accept that you will have to make tradeoffs among your various goals, the sooner you can move on to the task of getting your business to serve you.

Step One in the conflict resolution process is identifying goals that have a mandatory precedence over other goals. Sometimes there are things that must be done before other goals can be pursued.

For example, if one of your goals is to develop greater personal liquidity, it is mandatory that your business be strong enough and healthy enough before you can afford to take cash out of it. If the analysis of your business has shown that it is not strong enough,

> One characteristic of business owners that causes them much stress is their desire to find perfect solutions to conflicts between goals. Such solutions are rarely attainable. A significant percentage of the time there is no perfect solution— only tradeoffs.

then the business goals need to be attended to first.

In this case, the conflict between business goals and personal goals is reconciled by accepting a tradeoff. In the near term, the goal of personal liquidity must be put to one side. The primary goal and focus for the use of cash flow must first be on developing the strength of the business. Once that is accomplished, cash flow will be available for the second goal, developing personal liquidity.

If you discover mandatory goals, you may have already reconciled your conflicts and will be in a position to establish targets and action plans. Nevertheless, it is quite likely that your conflicts will not be so readily reconciled. Furthermore, establishing a clear hierarchy among your goals will require that you make personal value judgments. This is the part of the process that may be the most difficult for you since these decisions are subjective rather than objective in nature.

To make progress at this point, I suggest you accept a number of guiding principles for resolving conflicts between goals:

- First, as stated above, accept that there is no perfect answer, only tradeoffs. This means that you will not be able to achieve 100 percent of your goals.
- Second, no one can tell you what is right for you. You are the only judge of what is going to make you happy.
- Third, make a decision. The only way ultimately to reconcile a conflict between goals is to decide that one is more important to you than another. If you have come all the way to this point and fail to make the necessary critical decisions, you have wasted all the time and effort you have invested in the process.

Once you have completed the process of evaluating your goals and have made your decisions based upon both mandatory goals and goals that you have reconciled using your own value system, make a record of your hierarchy of goals.

Congratulations! You have created a framework designed to meet your personal needs, and now you are on your way to having your business serve you.

YOUR *SHORTCUTS TO SECURITY:*

- It is more often the rule than the exception that goals are not harmonious. Pursuing one goal often means having to give up another.
- These conflicts between goals tend to concentrate in three areas: conflicts related to the use of financial resources, conflicts related to the use of time and energy, and conflicts between desired end results.
- Conflicts must be reconciled in order to achieve meaningful change or improvement of personal situation.
- Resolving conflicts between goals often means making tough decisions as well as skillful compromises.

PART THREE

The Shortcut Revealed:

Your Payoff Awaits

CHAPTER NINE

Now That You Know Where You Want to Go, How Do You Get There?
• Establishing Targets
• Developing Action Plans

Earlier in this book I used the analogy of building a house. With the completion of the goal-setting portion of your *Shortcut to Security*, you now have an artist's rendering of what your *house* (what you want to get from business ownership) will look like. Though you've taken a step in the right direction, as was true with our homebuilder, a picture of your goals will not be sufficient for obtaining the desired results.

Translating the artist's rendering into a tangible home will require a blueprint that details exactly what is required to construct the edifice. For you to achieve the goals you have set for your business and yourself, you will also need a blueprint. to turn this picture into a reality.

Creating your own blueprint will require establishing specific targets for future action, detailing the specific action plans necessary to achieve each target, and managing the entire process to ensure that the actions are accomplished.

THE DIFFERENCE BETWEEN GOALS, TARGETS, AND ACTION PLANS

For the purposes of The Podolny Method©, we use these definitions:

- A goal is the ultimate end result that you wish to achieve. It is, in most cases, based on a personal, value-driven decision.
- A target is a specific accomplishment that must be achieved for a goal to become a reality. There may be a number of targets that must be fulfilled to reach a specific goal. There may also be a number of secondary targets needed to fulfill the requirements of a major target.
- Action plans are the specific train of sequential actions that must be completed to accomplish a target.

Let's look at an example to understand the differences. Assume that after having gone through the goal-setting process, you have identified an overall goal of exiting from your business. You have also identified a mandatory goal of improving the performance of the business in order to get enough from the sale to achieve personal financial independence.

The following is a list of targets (bullets) and secondary targets (arrows) that have been identified to improve business performance:

- Put into place professional senior management so that the potential buyer is not dependent on the owner for business performance after the sale of the business.
  - » Establish a senior management development program.
  - » Recruit and hire candidates for the senior management development program.
- Upgrade the financial controls of the business so that management can respond faster to critical variables that affect profitability.
  - » Acquire new internal accounting software.
  - » Retain a new outside accounting firm.
- Improve marketing and sales
  - » Develop marketing research capability so that the company knows where to best focus marketing in order to better identify sales prospects.
- Improve the quality of the company's sales management program.

We now have a set of primary and secondary targets that must be accomplished if we are to achieve the mandatory goal of improving the performance of the business in anticipation of a sale. For each of these targets, it will be necessary to work out an action plan for reaching that target. The following is a sample action plan for the secondary target of retaining a new outside accounting firm:

- Develop a list of all the issues relating to the work of the current accounting firm that are the reason a new firm is being sought.
- Research a target list of firms to be contacted.
- Contact the firms.
- Conduct initial meetings with the firms.
- Based upon the initial meetings, prune the list of prospects and solicit bids for work.
- Review the bids.
- Contact references provided by the bidding accounting firms.
- Choose the new accounting firm.
- Develop a new action plan for implementing the change.
- Execute the action plan necessary to actually accomplish the change.

THE VALUE OF PLANNING OVER JUST HAVING A PLAN

I am an ardent believer in the use of planning. But I am a less enthusiastic proponent of formal business plans. Clearly there are a number of business situations where a formal business plan is either required or desirable.

Companies that are in the high-tech industry and wish to tap the venture capital market must have a formal written business plan to be considered credible. As businesses get larger,

All too often, a written plan becomes an end unto itself, sitting on a shelf, having failed in its objective to provide a usable framework for ongoing decision-making.

written documents can assist in communicating and clarifying goals and objectives.

Yet all too often, even in larger businesses, a written plan becomes an end unto itself, sitting on a shelf, having failed in its objective to provide a usable framework for ongoing decision-making.

This is why I am a strong proponent of the implementation of ongoing planning procedures. The operative word is "ongoing." Planning should not be an event that takes place outside of the main activities of the business. It should not be a once-a-year event and then forgotten until the next year. It should be a living, breathing process that is a part of business operations.

Planning involves looking ahead, anticipating what needs to be done, and taking the appropriate action to see that what you have planned gets done. Planning as a continuous activity as opposed to a static plan takes into account that the business environment is always changing. It also takes into account that the results of our planning may not turn out exactly the way we projected. Therefore, the planning process itself needs to have the ability to change, alter course, and make adjustments.

When I work with clients, there is generally a rhythm to the planning process. You will also observe this as you go through the process described in this book. As you go from goals to targets to action plans, you will devote substantial time to the planning process. Yet as you move into the initiation and accomplishment of specific tasks, you will move away from planning and into action.

> *Planning should not be an event that takes place outside of the main activities of the business. It should be a living, breathing process that is a part of business operations.*

There comes a time when planning needs to be put into reality. The blueprint is finished, and it's time to build. Of course, from time to time business owners need to go back to the conclusions draws from the planning process to measure the progress of the action, just as the builder periodically checks his blueprints. As targets are reached, the planning process should be reviewed and new targets established.

STRATEGIC PLANNING AND TACTICAL PLANNING

There are different levels of planning. When you set your goals, you are involved with strategic planning. These are the overriding objectives that you want to achieve to get your business to serve you. When you start developing specific, short-term action plans to achieve targets, you are involved in tactical planning.

Strategic planning is something that is done from time to time. You should always have your vision "out there," but it should not be the dominant focus of your time use. On the other hand, tactical planning is something that is a part of your everyday management, measuring results against plans, readjusting plans, issuing new instructions, measuring results again, and so on.

YOUR *SHORTCUTS TO SECURITY:*

- Identifying the conflicts between goals and making reconciling decisions is only a start. There must be a means to turn these decisions into action.
- Building an Action Plan requires that you break down the requirements for achieving a goal into a logical sequence descending from general to specific.
- Building your Action Plan should be thought of in terms of ongoing planning. as opposed to merely writing a business plan.
- Planning needs to be consistently reviewed and updated as circumstances change. It is not a document that sits on a shelf.

CHAPTER TEN

The Key to the Shortcut—*Doing,* Initiating, and Pushing Action by Focusing Small

There are two critical aspects to successfully implementing a program that will transform your life with your business and transform the business itself so that it serves your needs. The first of these is the planning process that we have just completed. Until you know where you are going and what actions are required to get where you want to go, your efforts will be aimless.

Yet once you have direction, it is essential to take action and do all the things necessary to make your plan a reality. Taking the actions necessary to transform a plan into reality is a significant stumbling block for many business owners. I have made overcoming this block a major focus of my consulting practice. Why? Because the laws of physics apply to human endeavors as well as physical forces.

Your business has inertia. It is a mass of activity, but that activity likely is taking it in a single direction. You, the business owner, must overcome the inertia of your own habitual behavior as well as the habitual behaviors of the rest of the people in your business. As any student of human behavior can relate, getting people to change is difficult. And the reason many plans for businesses fail is that people do not

> *Once you have direction, it is essential to take action and do all the things necessary to make your plan a reality.*

have an effective method for overcoming that resistance to change.

What process can we use, therefore, to overcome this built-in human inertia (resistance to change) and achieve the ultimate success that we are looking to attain?

THE PHYLLO DOUGH METHOD: LAYERING SMALL, EASY-TO-ACHIEVE ACTIONS IN ORDER TO PROMOTE CHANGE

I have dubbed the method I use to effectively promote change and accomplish actions "The Phyllo Dough Method." Phyllo dough, if you are not familiar with it, is a Greek pastry dough that comes in extremely thin sheets. A single sheet of phyllo dough by itself is almost inconsequential. But if many of these sheets of phyllo dough are layered, wonderful culinary creations can result.

My method follows a similar principle. The key to initiating successful change is to break down actions into pieces that are small enough to be easily accomplished. People focus best on accomplishing one small action at a time. When the first small action is accomplished then a second action is assigned and accomplished and so on. You can use this process as an individual, or it can be used to manage a group. To make this process work, it is essential to do the following:

- Establish a regular time where the progress of the project being undertaken will be reviewed. This can be weekly or biweekly. Periods much longer than two weeks do not provide rapid enough feedback to achieve the desired change in inertia. These meetings do not have to be long. In fact, it is preferable that they be short and to the point.
- Use someone as a facilitator, preferably someone who is not actively involved with the particular group responsible for the actions. One of the requirements of this method is blunt honesty regarding who is accomplishing or not accomplishing assigned actions. Such feedback is much more likely to be provided by someone who is outside of the group responsible for the actions. It is also important to have a facilitator if you

are also involved in making the changes. If all of us were good at changing our own patterns, we would not need to be going through the process in the first place.

- Have the facilitator document each meeting, showing exactly what actions have been assigned to which person and when that action is supposed to be completed. Document any changes in disposition of the actions. If an action is completed, note it. If the action is still open, note it. Continue moving your business forward out of its inertia by crediting those who accomplish tasks.

The process of scheduling regular meetings, assigning specific actions to specific people, setting deadlines for accomplishment, and documenting progress becomes a powerful force for change. Initially one can expect skepticism from the participants. Yet as actions are accomplished—one after the other—those same participants will soon recognize that real progress is being made. Once that occurs, people are usually won over to the process. My clients are often amazed that after as little as three months, we have already accomplished significant portions of the actions required to attain their targets and goals.

YOUR *SHORTCUTS TO SECURITY*:

- How do you make your planning a reality? By taking action.
- Taking action requires discipline, control, and continuity.
- Focus not on the totality of the plan, but on the specific actions that are required to start work on the plan.
- As the first set of specific actions are completed, work on the next set of actions. Before long you will find that you have made significant progress toward your goals.

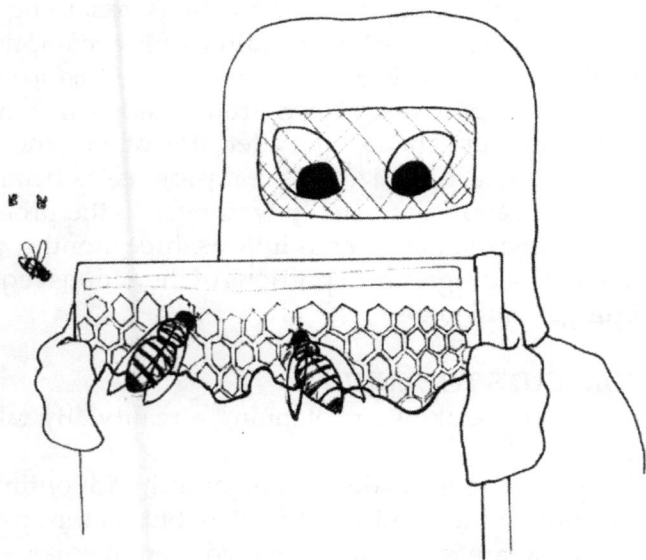

CHAPTER ELEVEN

Turning Your Business Activity into Financial Independence – Part 1
Quantify • Target • Save

There are only two ways to create wealth from a privately-held business. Shocking, isn't it? Only two. The first is to take advantage of the ability of a private business to produce high cash-on-cash rates of return (the amount of cash earnings produced each year compared to the net worth of the business) and the other is by realizing a capital gain by the sale of the business (to either outsiders or insiders).

In this chapter we will focus on the cash earnings of your business. In Chapter Twelve we will focus on the sale of your business to outsiders, and in Chapter Thirteen we will focus on a sale to insiders.

Principles for building wealth by saving earnings:

1. Calculate the amount you need to achieve financial independence and when you want to achieve it (see Chapter Seven and Appendix C).

> *It is highly likely that the sale of your business is not going to provide for 100 percent of the earning power you have received from your business.*

2. Establish annual targets for the amount that needs to be put away to achieve this goal.

3. *Plug in the amount that needs to be taken out of the business annually and make sure it is one of the goals of your business planning.* **This needs to be as important as growth or any other business goal!!!!!**

4. Set up a tax-advantaged savings program (a complicated subject) even if small. The earlier the better.

So far you've learned how to define your financial and business goals, how to evaluate your business, and how to develop a plan of action in order to achieve those goals.

Now, prepare to be hit between the eyes with a two-by-four. There is nothing more important in the book than this:

It is highly likely that the sale of your business is not going to provide for 100 percent of the earning power that you have received from your business.

You have to *save* in addition to trying to maximize the value of your business, otherwise you will not have the security you desire. It's just that simple.

As was discussed in Chapter One, there are only two ways to create wealth in privately held businesses. The first is taking advantage of the ability of a private business to produce high cash-on-cash rates of return. That is, the amount of cash earnings produced each year compared to the net worth of the business. The other is by realizing a capital gain through the sale of the business to either outsiders or insiders.

In Table 1 from Chapter One, Lesson Two you were shown how the players in the "deal business," the business of buying and selling businesses, are going to look at a company and derive a value for it:

THIS IS NOT ROCKET SCIENCE.

It's about discipline.

It's about planning.

TABLE 1
Calculation of Cash Flow:

Income before taxes	$250,000
Plus:	
Surplus Owner's Compensation	50,000
Adjusted Income before taxes	$300,000
Plus:	
Depreciation	200,000
Cash Flow or IBITDA	$500,000

Remember how our business owner was given the benefit of the doubt for the sale of his business? He was given a splendid price equal to five times his cash flow, a significant premium over average multiples. That gave the business owner $2.5 million.

The $2.5 million sounds like a lot of money, but there are some things the owner is going to have to account for. Of course, he has to pay taxes. If taxes are 20 percent, he will be left with $2 million. If he has no other investments, this is what the business owner will have available to support his lifestyle from now on. A prudent financial manager may tell this business owner that an earnings rate of 5 percent on his nest egg is a conservative and safe number. At 5 percent this owner will earn $100,000 per year.

So, this business owner has gone from a $250,000 income to a $100,000 income, *even though he sold his business at a significant premium…which is very optimistic and probably not realistic in the first place.*

Myth: If you transform the market value of your business into a financial investment asset, it will adequately cover your financial security needs.

Reality: If you transform the market value of your

business into a financial investment asset, it most likely will <u>not</u> cover the level of income you have enjoyed as a business owner.

So how do you fill the gap? You fill the gap by *saving.*

By looking at this example, you understand that you may be taking—under the best of circumstances—a 50 percent hit in your earning power when you sell your business for a relatively full and fair price. You are going to have to make that up by building up assets from the earnings of the company. Fortunately, well run privately held businesses that do the things discussed in the early chapters of this book will create an excellent cash-on-cash rate of return. If you will simply not spend it all, and if you start saving it on a regular and controlled basis, you can ensure that you will have the capital you need to have the security you want.

Once again, THIS IS NOT ROCKET SCIENCE. It's about discipline. It's about planning. So how do you do it? What are the principles that you need to follow to build wealth this way? First of all, you must figure out how much you will need. You need to say, "I want financial independence five years from now" or ten years from now or twenty years from now. "I need to know how much that independence will cost. How much am I going to spend in rent? How much for housing? How much am I going to spend in cars? Am I going to have an extra home?"

You can use the form found in Appendix C to calculate those figures.

Once you have your projections, you can figure out how much you must accumulate over time to ultimately provide that kind of income outside of your business.[1] A rough rule of thumb—in terms of a gross estimate of what to aim for—is that 5 percent of your assets should equal the after-retirement income you are looking for.

Now that you know what that number is and how long you must save to achieve it, you can go back and determine how much you need to be taking out of your business (to put in savings and investments) in order to be able to fulfill that goal.

---

[1] It is advisable to obtain the services of a certified financial planner in order to estimate more correctly what assets you will need to accumulate to ensure your financial security.

If you are very early in your business career, you might say, "I can't possibly save that much. I don't make enough money today to do that." But you can certainly start toward the goal. If you are further along in your business, you might take a much closer look at where you are spending money, determine where else you need to be spending, and where you can free up available cash to put away.

Whatever number comes up—whether that number needs to be growing over a long period of time or whether it needs to be a large number to put away over a short period of time because you are already much closer to your goal—that number, that savings amount, now needs to become a target that you put into the written goals of your business planning. Your business plan needs to include, in addition to funding, operations, reinvestment, and all the other normal business things, a plan for producing X amount of additional cash flow that you can take out of the business and put into a savings vehicle.

Having a savings plan for your business is as important as growth or any other business goal, because it is what creates shareholder value.

There are a number of different ways to accomplish this goal. We start out with "qualified savings vehicles," retirement savings plans that are government-approved under ERISA regulations, which were referred to earlier. These allow you to put away a certain amount of dollars based upon what you are offering other people in your company. All these dollars are pre-tax dollars, so that as long as you are making profits, you want to take advantage as much as possible of pre-tax income. You want to save yourself some taxes.

As companies make more and more money, more options become available under ERISA for sophisticated plan designs that will allow a business owner to take out a substantially greater portion of dollars to put away in savings vehicles. This is called top-heavy discriminatory planning, meaning that it favors those who make more money and who are in an ownership position within a business.

This is a complicated subject, so we will not go into detail here. You should obtain the services of a retirement plan designer who specializes in top-heavy discriminatory plans. Typically, third-party administrators—that is, those who administrate retirement plans—often have plan designers and may be able to give you a referral. You are looking for people who are specialists in the area of top-heavy discriminatory planning as opposed to people who are associated with large investment companies or insurance companies.

Once you have the necessary assets, then you need to invest them. That, again, is in the purview of investment advisors. Investment advising is another complicated subject on which people have written entire books, meaning that you must find a good quality conservative asset manager. Typically, the people who design plans are not the people who invest money.

But remember—this is important—you're taking risk in your business. The purpose of the money you are taking *out* of your business and putting aside is not to get the same kind of return on investment that you get *in* your business. Yes, it is to grow that money, but it's also to protect that money, so we advise conservatism when investing these assets.

If you have maxed out what you can do under the rules of a qualified plan, then there are non-qualified plans. These are typically insurance or annuity-based products that allow you to invest dollars that you have already paid taxes on, which can accumulate over time, tax-deferred. There have been tremendous improvements in these products in recent years. The insurance industry has recognized the investment needs of the Baby Boomer generation, who typically have their money in 401(k)-type investments, to have the features of a pension plan, meaning a future guaranteed cash flow stream.

Again, we recommend that people find someone who is a generalist, who is not tied to any particular insurance company or family of products, and who can explain to you the plusses and minuses, advantages and disadvantages, of various types of products out there.

Further, it is very important to recognize in both qualified and non-qualified plans that there are no perfect solutions, that there are always certain tradeoffs. For example, if you want to get the best out of a quailfied plan, you may have to give more to your employees than you may have thought about in order to get the benefits of the more discriminatory treatment Or, if you want to take advantage of a guaranteed flow of income down the road, you may be giving up some growth potential. The best advisors will show you such plusses and minuses so that you can make an informed decision.

YOUR *SHORTCUTS TO SECURITY*:
- Quantify the total amount you need to achieve financial independence and the amount of time it will take you to save it.
- Target the amount you will need to save annually from the profits of your business in order to meet your goals for financial independence.
- Using a qualified financial planner, determine how you will save and invest these funds, apart from your business, always keeping in mind that the ultimate goal is to have your business serve you.

CHAPTER TWELVE

Turning Your Business Activity into Financial Independence – Part 2
Optimizing the Results of a Business Sale

The subtitle of this book is *Make Your Business Worth More to You*©.

Yet very few businesses have the potential for earning a premium value during a sale. In fact, many business owners (actually a shockingly large number) take actions over the life of their ownership that reduce the value of their business and, in some cases, make the business unsalable.

There are numerous reasons why the value of a business may be reduced. One of the most significant is the psychological nature of buyers. They are typically intelligent and have been successful. They don't part with their money frivolously; they are cautious and definitely don't want to overpay for anything. They expect a reasonable, if not superior, rate of return on their investment. A four- to five-year payback period on a business acquisition investment would be a normal expectation.

> *Very few businesses have the potential for earning a premium value during a sale. In fact, many business owners (actually a shockingly large number) take actions over the life of their ownership that reduce the value of their business and, in some cases, make the business unsalable.*

WHAT IS CONSIDERED *AVERAGE*
WHEN PRICING A BUSINESS?

In this regard, *average* refers to the marketplace of middle-sized, privately-held businesses. These are businesses that range in sales of $3 million to $50 million. In my nearly thirty years of deal-doing, the vast majority of the transactions that I have closed (more than $500 million) have fallen into a rather tight pricing range. That price range has been a multiple of four to five times Income before Interest, Taxes, Depreciation and Amortization (IBITDA), with IBITDA adjusted for reasonable items, such as owner compensation above replacement salary level and one-time, non-reoccurring investment expenditures. If doing a calculation of payback on investment, this formula will lead to the four- to five-year payback period mentioned in the previous paragraph (assuming IBITDA remains the same).

When planning, I suggest business owners average the last three years of their IBITDA for a rough estimate of value. In today's market this initial value, based upon the multiple of IBITDA, is often called the *Enterprise Value* of the business. Any existing debt is deducted from the Enterprise Value to derive the net proceeds before taxes to the seller.

CONDITIONS THAT CREATE
OPPORTUNITY FOR A PREMIUM

It usually takes a convergence of factors for a business to reasonably expect to earn a premium above average valuation. Occasionally, extraordinary market conditions (remember dot-coms and telecommunications?) temporarily put an industry in a position to earn significant premiums:

> **Superior Performance** - First and foremost, a business sets the stage to gain a premium price by being a top performer in its industry. Performance is defined by profitability compared to others in the industry along with sales and profit growth.

Trend - Performance should be improving. Sales and profits should have grown in the past and have the prospect of continuing to grow.

Market Opportunity - There should be a perception that good things are in store for businesses in your industry.

Scarce Commodity - You have some advantage such as technology, process, market share, etc., that is expensive to duplicate or compete against.

Buying Frenzy - Suddenly some subset of buyers or investors feel they have to be in your industry, and start buying everything in sight.

The best opportunity to earn a premium exists when everything is going right for a business and its industry, and when the perception is that it will continue to do well in the future.

Very rarely do the factors that create a premium opportunity last for long periods of time. These opportunities to achieve a valuation premium during a sale are typically short-lived windows of opportunity. It may seem extremely counter-intuitive to sell during such a positive environment, but I have known many owners who have regretted not taking advantage of such windows.

> *The best opportunity to earn a premium exists when everything is going right for a business and its industry, and when the perception is that it will continue to do well in the future.*

CONDITIONS THAT CREATE DISCOUNTS
OR AN INABILITY TO SELL

The pendulum can often swing the other way, leading to a business being valued at less than average or being unable to find a buyer at all. Here are some of the many reasons that the value of a business may be discounted below average:

Erratic or Negative Performance - When profits are inconsistent, buyers will tend to value a business based upon the valleys, not the peaks. When profits decline, buyers disappear.

Negative Market Conditions - If your industry is in a decline, there is going to be little interest, even if your particular business is doing well.

Poor Records, Accounting, Systems, and Controls - If the quality of information you provide to buyers is poor, they will assume it is inaccurate; as a result, they will discount the price they are willing to pay, or they will look elsewhere for lower risk opportunities.

Over-Dependence upon the Owner for Company Performance - When buyers perceive the success of a business is a function of the owner's personal involvement and activities, they reasonably assume the business will lose much of its performance once the owner is cashed out and gone.

Clearly, gaining a realistic estimation of business value allows you to create a more realistic exit strategy and is a crucial element of your personal financial planning.

PREPARING FOR A SALE
Start Your Planning Well in Advance

Most sellers I work with make one simple but significant error. They wait much too long to begin the process of readying themselves to sell. For many business owners it seems as if many factors, which were previously below the conscious level, suddenly emerge all at once and lead the owner to decide it is time to sell. It is not unusual for the owner to then come to me and request help in selling their business with the expectation we can conduct a successful sale in a matter of months!

Sellers need to start much earlier in their planning if they are to achieve the best results in the sale of their business.

Sellers need to start much earlier in their planning if they are to achieve the best results in the sale of their business. Buyers typically look at three to five years of the financial history and records of a business. The factors that cause a discounted value can take years to rectify. Therefore, the seller who wants to maximize price and marketability will start taking appropriate action years in advance.

Make Financial Performance and Reporting as Attractive as Possible

Here is a simple rule. Make it easy for the buyer to see how much money you make. Saving taxes and improving cash flow drive many business owners' financial reporting decisions at the expense of reporting profits. Buyers are not going to spend effort digging to find your profits. While some restatement of profitability is common, such as accounting for excess owner's compensation, the less that needs to be done the better.

Second, the trend is your friend. You want to be presenting an "up" trend in earnings if possible, or at least consistent earnings. Erratic or "down" trends in earnings are going to have a seriously negative impact on your value and marketability.

Third, you also want to have the best quality financial statements you can afford and have them for a number of years. I know many business owners who hate to spend money on their year-end financial statements. Instead, they use simple compilations done on a tax basis with little or no disclosure. This type of statement provides no credibility when it is time to sell. It sends red flags to buyers, telling them they should take the financial information they have received with a big grain of salt.

When preparing to sell, you want to provide full disclosure

statements, with footnotes and complete schedules. Your numbers should be as close to generally accepted accounting principles (GAAP) as possible. A review-quality statement is substantially better than a compilation, and an audited statement is ideal.

Your Tax Homework

Meet with your advisors and understand the tax consequences of a buyer purchasing assets, since the vast majority of transactions are asset purchases rather than purchases of stock. Research any changes you can make that will enhance your after-tax return of a transaction. In some cases there are advantages to making such changes well in advance of a business sale.

Clean Up Legal Documentation

Not all owners are diligent about maintaining the legal background documentation of their businesses. Often, formal corporate governance requirements such as filings, board of directors meetings, and shareholder approvals are lacking. It is not always easy to find contracts, leases, and other important documents when they are needed on short notice.

When preparing to sell, have your legal records reviewed by an attorney experienced in business sales, as if he were doing due diligence for a buyer. This will give you time to remedy any deficiencies before you bring the company to market.

Document Your Processes and Procedures

The way you conduct business is your secret to success. If that information is locked in your head or your people's, it represents a risk for the buyer. What will the buyers do if you or some of your people leave after they buy the business? Creating written processes and procedures institutionalizes this information, reducing buyer risk and increasing the value of the business being sold.

Reduce Dependence on the Owner

The more your business success depends upon the current owner's personal work and contribution, the more risk buyers will perceive. After all, if they give you enough money so you don't have to work, are you going to be as motivated as you were before? Owners who want to posture their business for sale should be working to replace what they do by developing others in the business.

Focusing well in advance on the goal of selling and taking the appropriate preparatory actions will put you in the best possible position to sell successfully.

EXECUTING THE SALE PROCESS
Common Problems Within
the Business Sale Process

The process of selling your business has the potential to take extraordinary amounts of your time and energy. Buyers can have you jumping through hoops, but then decide to take a pass based on information obvious in the very beginning. It is easy for the process to drag on and on, as one buyer after another goes through their dance of evaluation, each disrupting the normal flow of business operations. Here is the method I have used to close more than half a billion dollars in transactions. It is a method that makes the best use of your time, ensures you are exposed fully to the market, and enhances the conditions leading to the best price available.

Step 1: Creating a Package That Puts
Your Business in the Best Light

Before going to market, you should create a document that conveys to buyers the significant facts about your business. This allows the buyer to learn much, without having to be in direct contact with you.

Right from the start, your package should communicate the logical arguments for why your business is an attractive acquisition candidate. In addition, there should be enough tangible information for a buyer to tell if the proposed acquisition is a good fit or not, saving everyone time. A good package creates a basis for future credibility. While emphasizing the points of opportunity, avoid inaccurate information or data that cannot be confirmed later. Typical elements of a package include:

- Summary information on your industry, focusing on positive trends that indicate this business as a good acquisition opportunity.
- A history of the business, leading to the current positive reasons for buying it.
- A discussion of operations.
- The analysis of three to five years of financial information, highlighting positive trends and comparisons with your industry.
- A conclusion, tying the previous elements together into a logical argument for acquiring the business.

Step 2: Researching Potential Buyers

Based upon events occurring in your industry and in the economy, develop a thorough list of potential buyers. Consider databases such as Dun & Bradstreet or Standard & Poor's as well as industry newsletters and trade associations. You should also be sure to include the names of private equity groups and investors. Establish some initial screening criteria based upon the size of your business and the buying habits of those you are approaching.

Step 3: Presenting the Opportunity

On average, you can expect to have a list of up to four hundred buyer candidates. Only a small number of these will have any serious interest. The goal of the presentation process is to identify that group and get them to visit you at about the same time.

Write a brief one-page letter that describes the most pertinent points relating to the acquisition opportunity. Tell them they can receive a detailed package upon request. All the letters should be mailed simultaneously. A 10 percent response requesting a package is good.

Once respondents are sent the package, follow up in about two weeks to confirm receipt, to answer questions and to secure follow-up information requests. The goal is two-fold: Weed out non-serious or lowball buyers and get serious buyers to agree to visit as soon as possible. Try to avoid discussion of price unless impossible to do otherwise.

Step 4: Initial Visits

This is the critical moment—to get a buyer beyond rational evaluation. When a buyer develops a positive feeling about the people and the company, he enters the territory that leads to the best outcome for the seller. The goal is to get potential buyers interested in visiting the seller in the most compressed time possible. This minimizes the disruption and creates a competitive atmosphere.

You should make sure you have reviewed the package you sent out, because the buyers will be asking you questions already answered in the package as a test of its accuracy and consistency. Positive first visits will lead to requests for more information and often, second visits. The goal now is to get offers. Try to establish a deadline for receiving offers, if possible, without alienating quality buyers.

Step 5: Negotiation

Compare proposals. Conduct shuttle negotiations with buyers to develop the best possible offer.

Step 6: The Close

Once you have chosen a buyer proposal, you want to move as swiftly as possible to a close. Get the buyer to detail the due diligence process and set a timetable. If possible, avoid the letter of intent that is rarely binding, and go directly to a definitive agreement. The sooner the buyer starts spending money on legal and due diligence the better. Now the buyer has a tangible investment to lose if a closing does not occur. Beware emotional reactions. Don't kill your deal over an issue that heats your emotions but is only worth a couple of percentage points. Get to the closing.

YOUR *SHORTCUTS TO SECURITY:*

- Optimizing the results of the business sale process for building financial independence requires substantial preparation and an understanding of the "rules of the game."
- Most businesses sell within a very narrow trading range—four to five times the adjusted Income Before Interest, Taxes, Depreciation, and Amortization (IBITDA).
- Businesses must be very aware of those items that can make a business unmarketable and those that drive a premium.
- Use of an acquisition professional and using an organized process for bringing your company to market will enhance your chances for a superior outcome.

CHAPTER THIRTEEN

Turning Your Business Activity into Financial Independence – Part 3

Creating Value by Selling to Insiders

There are many business types where the logical buyers, the highest bidders and best candidates, may be found inside the company. Some of these are professional firms and other firms who are heavily dependent on people assets. Others are companies that don't want to or can't take advantage of the conditions that drive value in the sale of the business.

Others are owners who feel loyal to those who have provided the work that has led to the owner's success. Often in these situations the people inside the company are in a better position to recognize the potential value than an outsider. In these cases a succession transaction offers a great opportunity to the owner.

Succession can also be attractive to an owner because the transaction can be timed so that it is gradual, allowing the owner to maintain his wage-earning potential from the business over time rather than suddenly being forced to rely on the proceeds from the sale of the business. This can allow the owner to merge the savings strategy discussed in Chapter Eleven with his exit strategy.

Succession offers an entire range of opportunities and risks that allow business owners to design their ultimate security.

Business owners and their advisors often use the terms "succession" and "exit" interchangeably, but doing so can be a source of misunderstanding leading to undesired consequences. There is a difference between exiting a business and providing for succession. Succession offers an entire range of opportunities and risks that allow business owners to design their ultimate security.

The words exit and succession actually indicate very different paths with different requirements and outcomes.

The words exit and succession actually indicate very different paths with different requirements and outcomes. An "exit" is the process of leaving a business. You are seeking exit if you desire to be free of the time constraints and restrictions of business ownership, desire to do other things with your life, and are looking to translate your built up equity into funds *no longer at risk in your business.*

Taking an exit implies you are selling your business. It's gone; you don't have to worry about it any longer. Ideally, someone has given you cash. You don't have any risk anymore. If the new owner wants to rape and pillage the business, he rapes and pillages it. The main thing is that you got your money out of the deal.

GETTING OUT OR LEAVING A LEGACY

Succession, on the other hand, implies that people you have selected in some way, shape, or form, whether they are family members, people who have grown up in the business, or someone you have recruited from the outside—but people you have picked—are going to start taking over the management and ownership of the business. These are not outsiders, these are insiders.

"Succession" is the process owners use to ensure their business will continue on when they are no longer involved. You are seeking succession when your goals are expressed in terms of maintaining the distinct mission and personality of the business, you want your family or your employees to take over your business, and you look at the continuity of the business as a representation of your own continuity.

CAN YOU SELL YOUR BUSINESS?

First, it is important to know that some businesses are not very saleable under any circumstance. For example, there is no tradition of business sales for commercial general contractors, even if the business carries many hundreds of millions of dollars in sales volume. General contractors typically cannot get someone to buy their business for anything like a reasonable price. The reason for this is because the business is only as good as the last bid, so there is no goodwill that is bringing in business volume on an ongoing basis.

Professional firms are another example: accounting firms, architecture firms, interior decorating firms, law firms, etc. Sometimes you can find buyers for these, sometimes not. Inevitably when you sell those businesses, you very rarely get cash, so you are always taking significant risk in terms of the new owner paying you only so long as the business succeeds.

Additionally, if you own a business where you are very important, where you are key to the success of that business, it is not going to be highly saleable. In that situation, if you can develop successors from within, people who want to take over your business, they are the best buyers and will probably pay a higher price than the outside market. In essence, you are creating a situation where an inside person can become an owner, usually someone who would likely never have another opportunity to become a business owner.

On the plus side, this kind of succession gives someone who does not have a natural market for their business, or an owner who is very loyal to his employees, or an owner who doesn't want his business to be taken over by "just anybody," the option of having an insider take over, and probably at a better price. You may or may not get a better price—that depends on the circumstances—but in that situation, you do have more control.

So why doesn't everybody attempt succession? Because it's hard to do a succession transaction. There is a logical progression that has to be followed. First, you must ensure that the proposed successors can, in fact, become owners. Do they have the temperament? Do they fit the psychological profiles for risk-taking and going against the grain that we referred to in our opening chapters? Just because someone says he might want to buy the business doesn't mean he really can. You must test any potential successors

Second, there is the whole question of whether you as the owner are actually going to let go. Because succession doesn't occur instantly, there is no instant moment of closing where you say, "Okay, you were employees before, and you're owners now." Instead, the changeover is done whereby gradually more responsibility and authority is turned over to the successors, and the owner gradually lets go. We know that owners tend not to have that type of personality, so that's a potential impediment.

Finally, we have to actually create a transaction, a buy-sell arrangement. As the owner, you will likely end up financing that arrangement, which means you will still be taking risk.

On the flip side, a positive aspect of succession is that you are able to manage the entire transaction. Another advantage is that you can get out of your business on a gradual basis, so that as you are selling your stock bit by bit over time, you can still be earning money so that you don't immediately have to tap into the proceeds of the sale.

EMPLOYEES AND OWNERS— CUT FROM DIFFERENT MOLDS

Unfortunately, owners do not always take into account that there are major differences in the personality and motivations of owners and employees. Only a small percentage of employees ever step into the role of owner/entrepreneur. It takes a high degree of self-motivation and a willingness to accept risk to make that jump. That does not mean that there no employees who can make the transformation. Nevertheless, owners should be very careful, calculating the traits that are essential for someone succeeding them, then measure their employees to see if they have these traits.

> *It takes a high degree of self-motivation and a willingness to accept risk to make the jump from employee to owner.*

Always start with management succession by determining whether the successors have what it takes for ownership. Do the employees understand what an owner does? In an earlier chapter we referred to the fact that it is the owner who figures out what a problem is and then figures out how to solve it. In the process of succession transition, you, as the owner, will create circumstances where you can give your successor (or successor team) a problem. You will tell them to figure out the problem, come back to you with what they think the problem is, and then format a plan for solving the problem. Then you tell them to go ahead and resolve it.

Typically, that process takes six months to a year before the potential successors understand the ins and outs of ownership and before you can truly see that they are capable of owning your business. Unfortunately, a lot of employees will fail the first test. On average, we find that about 50 percent of the people who want to do a succession never get beyond this step.

Additionally, at some point during the transition process, you will need to educate your people regarding the financial realities of ownership. They need to understand that when push comes to shove, they are the ones who won't get paid. That they have to put their financial health on the line when they go to the bank to borrow the money. That while there is the opportunity to make a lot of money, there is also the chance for losing it all. It is very, very important that your potential successors understand what type of risk they are taking.

Once you have established that the managers have what it takes and are the kind of people who will accept risk, who can see what a problem is, can put together a plan of action, and follow through on the execution of that action, then you have to go through with them everything that the owner does. You must do a complete catalog of what the owner or owners do, and you must determine how you will lay that on your successors.

Very rarely will you find one person who can fill the owner's shoes. The successors may have to take some of the owner's jobs and delegate them to someone else. You may have a team of people to do those kinds of jobs. There may be expert knowledge you have that will have to be replicated. In other words, you must identify exactly what has to be taken over and who among the successors is capable of taking over each task.

CASE STUDY: MINING COMPANY

The owner of this business had built a large, rapidly growing mineral extraction business. He was very dynamic, combining an excellent grasp of the operational requirements of his industry with a well-honed sense for deal doing.

Two years after the closing of this transaction the new owners decided to liquidate the company and sold it in pieces to various others in the industry. What went wrong?

He had built his business by acquiring underperforming assets from corporate sellers and turning them around with much leaner overhead structures.

As he grew his company, he built an impressive team of bright, professional managers. At the height of his success, this owner went through a reevaluation of his own objectives.

He decided to sell the business. While he could have found a buyer on the outside, it was his great desire to see his management team step into his shoes. He arranged the entire transaction: getting appraisals, obtaining financing that did not overly strap the company, and setting his managers up with proper representation.

Two years after the closing of this transaction the new owners decided to liquidate the company and sold it in pieces to various others in the industry. What went wrong? The owner failed to take into account the importance of the intangibles he had brought to the business: his innate leadership qualities, creativity, and most importantly his tolerance for risk. His managers had been excellent when working with him, but they could not replicate those skills. Their inability to take risk in making decisions caused them to delay in a number of situations where expedient action was called for. Because they lacked the self-confidence of the founder, these former employees could not will themselves through the hard times as the original owner had done many times in the past.

Finally, there was no one real leader. At some point, the managers/new owners stopped being a team and became a dysfunctional set of factions. The owner had made a critical error in doing the transaction for the employees. He never allowed them to measure their own desire and appetite for risk. In fact, he had set them up to fail.

Succession is one of the most difficult outcomes for privately owned businesses to achieve. Owners must adopt a fiduciary role towards the successor employees. They should recognize the unique characteristics an owner must have to be successful. They must resist the temptation to simply hand a company to employees. They should create scenarios where the employees must show the drive, initiative and appetite for risk that any entrepreneurial owner must have to succeed. In doing so the owner will fulfill his fiduciary role and ensure that the new owners have the greatest opportunity for success.

STEPS TO A SUCCESSFUL SUCCESSION

In the natural progression of business ownership succession, management succession must precede ownership succession. You can have management succession and not have ownership succession. In fact, if you have management succession, and if— let's just say—the managers do not want to take on the financial risk of ownership, we have actually made our business more valuable (see Chapter Twelve).

Whereas you can have management succession without ownership succession, the inverse is not true. If you do not have successful management succession, then you definitely cannot have ownership succession, because there will be nobody to run the business.

Yet building and executing a successful succession plan is one of the most difficult tasks to accomplish in business. Many owners experience extreme frustration when trying to execute succession plans and even abandon them after many years of effort. The roots of these frustrations lie in the complicated succession plan process. Succession plans require the use of many different coordinated disciplines. Some disciplines may be completely new to the owner, while others may require a style and substance opposite to the owner's nature. The key to overcoming these challenges and achieving a successful succession plan is detailed implementation planning.

A PLAN OF ACTION

Once you have identified exactly what it is that you, as the owner, need to pass on to your successors, you next need to build an action plan, as identified earlier in The Podolny Method©. You will create an action plan with time tables for how you will, step by step, pass on various responsibilities. For yourself, not your successors, this is "Test No. 2." There will be owners who will say they want to pass these things on, but in fact will not. This is the second area where you will find that succession processes fall apart.

Step No. 3 is putting together the actual transaction. So you are in the place in the process where you have an individual or a group of people who have shown they have what it takes to be owners. You have already begun to give up responsibilities to them. At some point they will want to take over, and you then have to build a transaction.

You then have to ask: What is the value of the business? How much will I require for a down payment? How will the successors pay for over time? What kind of guarantee will there be? This gets into the whole world of "deal-doing," which is another complicated subject and another area where professional advice is required. You can also find myriad of books written on the subject, which we will not going to go into right now other than to say it is a very creative process, and there are many opportunities for win/win situations between both the successor and the owner.

CASE STUDY: OWNER'S STRUGGLE

The company was quite successful. It had an attractive trend of growing sales and earnings. Plus, with a good mix of capabilities it was well positioned for future growth. The owner had long-intended to sell the business to his key managers; however, they had come to an impasse over price and terms. The company's long-time corporate attorney had been asked to assist in structuring the transaction, but now found himself in an uncomfortable position. He recommended my services as an intermediary.

I began the process by uncovering the owner's motivations and comparing them to the characteristics of an exit and a succession.

The owner was clearly unsure of his desires. Despite his wish to sell the business to his key people, he believed the business deserved a premium price. I explained to him that the reason his key people could not possibly pay the premium he was seeking was because they were dependent upon the cash flow of the business to pay for the acquisition. Understanding this conflict and realizing his key people were acting in a rational manner diffused much of the tension.

> *The owner needed to make a choice between two conflicting goals.*

The owner needed to make a choice between two conflicting goals. He needed to discover what the market would actually offer for his business. We explained to the key managers the reasons for the decision. While they were disappointed, they logically understood the importance of sales price to the owner. Again this relieved some of the pressure.

We were able to solicit a number of proposals for substantially more than management could pay. However, the owner was unhappy with the proposals, because they would have resulted in some of the management team being removed. He therefore ultimately decided to take the lower price and go back to the original transaction with management. The transaction proceeded smoothly to closing.

Getting the owner to understand that he had both succession and exit goals, was the first step to resolution. The second step was his understanding that the solution for one goal (passing the business on) was not compatible with the other (getting the highest price to ensure future lifestyle). Fully exploring both options allowed the owner to reconcile the tradeoffs necessary to come to a resolution he felt comfortable with.

The desire to see the business you have built from scratch or inherited from your parents continue beyond your ownership is one of the most prevalent emotions among owners of successful businesses. Many owners go to great lengths to give their employees the opportunity to succeed them in the ownership of the business. Clearly, understanding the differences between objectives and solutions in succession and exit strategies prior to initiating action will lead to a more efficient and conflict free process.

CASE STUDY:
SHEET METAL PRODUCTS MANUFACTURER

The owner of a supplier of sheet metal components founded his business twenty-five years earlier. Upon entering his sixties, he was ready to step down from active involvement in the business. He had a strong paternalistic interest in the company and its employees. He had worked three years to implement a succession plan without success; he was frustrated.

My interviews of the owner and his managers provided an understanding of the issues. The owner was implementing a wide variety of succession-related programs that lacked consistency. He constantly shifted emphasis from one program to another in a seemingly random fashion. Management was losing faith in the entire concept of succession. It was clear he lacked an understanding of how the methods he was utilizing fit into the overall requirements of a successful succession plan.

I suggested we start by clearly defining the end result and working backward with increasing detail until we had a coordinated, step-by-step plan for the succession. We began by clarifying exit verses succession goals. We then established a list of programs which needed to be in place to achieve those goals:

- personal financial planning to quantify exit dollars required
- documentation of company vision, missions and values
- definition of key competencies and qualities required of the management replacing the owner
- evaluation of existing current management against required competencies and qualities
- programs for pushing decision making from the owner to the management team
- development, installation, and utilization of controls and reporting mechanisms
- testing management performance

- designing and executing the actual succession transaction

My client then understood each step and how the process would eventually produce the desired result. Still, he had some trepidation regarding the magnitude of the proposed project. We sought outside assistance in project management methodology to the plan, which provided the owner with the help he needed to keep the plan moving. Though it required three years, he ultimately had the pleasure of seeing his chosen (and proven) management team close on the succession purchase of his company.

Without a doubt, the completion of a successful succession transaction is difficult. Realizing the undertaking is a complex project that can be broken down into component parts allows the owner to address the intricate process in a methodical fashion. Approaching each component at the appropriate time prevents the owner from becoming overwhelmed and increases the opportunity for success.

FAMILY SUCCESSION PLANS

Distributing ownership of a family business to one's heirs can be an equally strong desire. It is motivated by a perception that the business is an important component of the family and by the desire to treat all heirs equally in terms of the wealth being inherited. These are worthy motivations. Unfortunately, there are cases where the unintended result of that desire is conflict among family members and feelings of being short-changed.

FAMILY IS NEVER A HOMOGENEOUS GROUP

Your potential heirs are all different people with different personalities. They have different financial situations. Their roles and eventual involvement with the business will be different. They will have different relationships among one another. Hence, they are by definition a heterogeneous group that may have conflicting goals. Yet some business owners fail to recognize these differences due to a desire to be fair and to keep the business in the family.

CASE STUDY:
CONTRACTOR WITH THREE CHILDREN

The owner had started with virtually nothing; he grew up in poverty and with little education. Yet over a thirty-year period he built an extremely successful specialty contracting business.

He had three children. One was his designated successor and second in command. Another worked in the bookkeeping department. The third was not active in the business. The owner had developed a succession plan that called for each of the three children to receive equal shares in the business via a program of gifting stock over time. I had been retained to assist in the development of a growth plan.

During the process, I became aware of problems between the siblings. The child in bookkeeping had a number of longstanding, deep-seated personal issues regarding the child designated as the future CEO. The inactive child was ambivalent about the business and really was not looking forward to any future involvement. I expressed my opinion to the father that his succession plan was likely a time bomb. When he was no longer there it could go off and easily tear the family apart.

I suggested the owner separate the goal of wealth transfer from the goal of business succession. This was achieved by having the child who would be managing the business acquire it from the father. Using outside valuations, we documented a price that was acceptable to all parties. The acquisition provided the father with liquid assets he could distribute to the other two children. The succession goal was achieved as well.

This example illustrates why business owners should carefully evaluate the ability of their heirs to work together before initiating plans to pass on ownership. Considering separating mechanisms for wealth transfer and succession for each heir should be included in the evaluation.

YOUR *SHORTCUTS TO SECURITY:*
- Value can often be created for difficult-to-sell businesses by grooming insiders or heirs as successors.
- What are the goals you have for your business? Do you want to sell it and gain the most you can for your financial security? Or is it more important to you to leave behind a legacy in the form of the business you have built?
- Succession takes a specific, often lengthy process. You must decide whether you want to exit your business or leave it to specific successors.

CHAPTER FOURTEEN

It's Up to You!

Earlier in this book, I made the statement that you, the owner, can achieve those things you truly wish from your business. This book provides you with the tools that I have used with many business owners to achieve just such results.

However, the best tools in the world are useless without the will to use them. The Podolny Method©, like methods found in other self-help texts, is only as effective as the person who is willing to implement it. As you take on the task of reinventing your business so it better serves you, here is a reminder of the key points that will make The Podolny Method© work for you.

YOUR *SHORTCUTS TO SECURITY*:

- Make a commitment. Your willpower is the first step to achieving change.
- Be disciplined. Set a specific, regular time each week to work on The Podolny Method© and don't expect miracles overnight.
- Consider using a third party to help you facilitate the process. Having someone with some distance from your day-to-day situation can be invaluable.
- Be honest with yourself. This is not the time to give answers that you think others expect of you.
- Accept that you may have to make some hard choices—there is rarely a perfect answer, only tradeoffs.

- Break down your goals into targets and action plans. Then break the required actions down even further into activities that can be realistically accomplished each week.
- Assign responsibilities and document the achievement of those responsibilities.
- Hold people accountable for the execution of action... especially yourself.

With commitment, honesty, and follow-through, your business can become the tool you have always wanted it to be for making your life full, happy, and prosperous.

CHAPTER FIFTEEN

Questions?
The Shortcut to Security Condensed

I am a consultant. I get paid to...anyone? Consult. Excellent. I get paid to consult. Exit and succession services are a strong field of focus.

The following excerpt from my website reads: *The culmination of private business life is an exit or succession that allows the owners to achieve full rewards for a lifetime of work. The Podolny Group provides a full range of service options from the initial examination of options available through the execution of specific strategies to assist the private business with the successful achievement of this most important of transitions.*

When I meet with a client, invariably there are a series of questions that come my way time and again. These are all excellent questions, and are presented as follows:

WHAT SKILLS AND PERSONAL TRAITS ARE ESSENTIAL IN ORDER TO SUCCESSFULLY START A NEW BUSINESS?

Owning a business is certainly not for everyone. If you do not have the skills and personal traits essential for starting a business, or if you do not quickly learn them, you are wasting your time. No surprise there. But what exactly are those skills and traits?

For one, you must be something of a risk taker. All right—you have to be a fairly big risk taker. You're doing this based on a somewhat intellectual gut feel. That is, your educated instincts tell you that working for "the man" is not necessarily the way to go. You're not necessarily going into this on the basis of all kinds of serious research. And if you did serious research, it's just research. It's not reality. You are still going to be taking tremendous risk.

So your typical entrepreneur, not surprisingly, is a risk taker. Who are *not* the risk takers? The people who tell you to work a solid nine-to-five job without taking into consideration that by doing so you barely have enough left over to survive and make your bills. It's the age-old conflict between the safe, take-no-risks attitude versus the willingness-to-take-risks attitude of most successful business owners.

When we do succession planning, the area where the proposed successors (perhaps the employees) who want to take over your business fail most often is in the same risk-taking aspect you understood when you started your business. As we undertake a succession planning engagement, the first thing we do at The Podolny Group is create a circumstance to see if the proposed successors will take risks. As it turns out, 75 percent will walk away from the transaction because of the risk. The reason why most people are employees is because they innately need that security and are unwilling to take on significant risk.

> *When we do succession planning, the area where the proposed successors fail most often is in the same risk-taking aspect you understood when you started your business.*

Secondly, besides being a risk taker, you must have a tremendous amount of self-confidence, because there is not a whole lot outside your own confidence that is justifying what you are doing. It is your belief in what you are doing that carries the show. Most everyone you know is going to tell you that you're crazy. And they're going to ask you, why don't you go get a job? You have to have the confidence to respond to these issues or to be able to ignore them.

Thirdly, you have to be a worker, and you have to be a self-motivated worker, be able to initiate things, and be able to see the problems and come up with solutions. You not only have to solve the problem, you have to figure out what the problem is. That really is what will put you in the category of an owner.

So, a concise description of a successful entrepreneur is a confident, risk-taking hard worker who is comfortable going against the grain while ignoring naysayers. They not only solve problems, but anticipate them. The typical entrepreneur can probably do whatever is required in the business extremely well, probably better than anybody else. They tend to be multi-faceted, and possess of unusual combinations of skill sets.

WHAT IS THE VALUE OF GOAL-SETTING?

The value of goal-setting is to establish a clear vision of what you would like to see happen at a future period in time, with sufficient enough detail, that you can track your vision back and create an action plan. In my experience, very few people really set goals, certainly not long-term goals. Their long-term goals, if any, tend to be extremely vague. Instead, people seem to be better at setting short-term goals. For example, *I need to do this in the next week or month*. This is what I call incremental planning and goal-setting.

I believe that for individuals or businesses to truly attain financial independence, they need to set both long-term and short-term goals. Of course, there will always be businesses and people who will happen to be in the right place at the right time with good fortune shining upon them almost in spite of themselves. Just the same, for these entities the financial independence they gain tends to dissipate shortly thereafter, because they did not take the time to plan out the future beyond their immediate good fortune.

As such, it is clear that goal-setting for both the long-term and the short-term is imperative.

HOW DO YOU CALCULATE WHAT YOU NEED
FOR FINANCIAL INDEPENDENCE?

Despite what most people think, it is not that difficult to calculate what one needs for financial independence. In reality, when we look at personal expenditures we find that most budgeted items fall within a relatively small number of categories—Housing, Medical Care, and Automotive. These three categories alone usually account for up to 60 percent of what a person spends. It doesn't take much more than going through a checkbook every three to four months to get an idea as to where things are going. You can extrapolate from there (see Appendix C for a Financial Independence Requirements Spreadsheet).

I'VE GOT ALL THESE KIDS GOING TO COLLEGE; WHEN DO I FINALLY ACHIEVE FINANCIAL INDEPENDENCE?

You need to plan and save when you are in your prime earning years. Don't wait to consider your financial independence until soon before you reach retirement age; it is important to begin planning and investing long before retirement. Don't make the mistake of assuming that the future sale of your business will provide a large enough payout that your financial requirements will be met. The majority of principals selling a business today will find that the proceeds from their sale will provide for much less continuing income than they earned when they owned the business.

Having said all this, I believe any business owner serious about building wealth and security should have a financial planning professional on his team of advisors. The difference between a good and a great outcome may be the knowledge that only a quality professional can provide.

WHAT HAS BEEN YOUR BIGGEST SURPRISE AS A SUCCESSION PLANNER?

Here is an eye-opening fact that I've learned from my years as head of The Podolny Group: The actual difference in the personal lifestyles of most business owners is very small, regardless of whether a company earns $2 million or $20 million annually. It's not like one owner spends $250,000 a year and another owner spends $600,000 a year. In fact, in my line of work, the vast majority of client-owners of multi-million dollar companies spend considerably less than $250,000 a year on their lifestyle, and frequently less than $150,000.

My point is, even if you are a new business owner and are still in the red, or you have yet to earn a dime from your business, there is no better time to consider these life lessons than now. If you start out prudently, think long-term, and always refer back to your business objectives, there is no reason why you cannot achieve your professional and personal goals.

Note that when taking into account your future financial needs, you must likewise take inflation into account. It is also important to understand that your money available for spending is an after-tax number. You need to calculate the pre-tax number that you need in order to yield this required *after-tax* amount. This reality requires that you be aware of your tax rate. In other words, if you have a $100,000 lifestyle and are in a 25 percent tax bracket, you will need to earn about $133,000 in after-tax income, in order to fund the $100,000 spending.

HOW CAN I SUCCEED IN MY QUEST FOR FINANCIAL INDEPENDENCE?

You start by being logical and calculating numerically what the outcome is going to be in any given circumstance. A theme throughout this book is that there are not an infinite number of ways to do things. I can't tell you the number of clients I have who consistently look for new solutions while ignoring the obvious.

People will say things such as, "That can't be right. We need to dig deeper. There must be something else. There must be some other thing we're missing." There are a large number of people who seem to feel that there's a magic bullet that suddenly gets you to a point where you are making tons of money, and that people will throw money at your business. I constantly fight this battle in terms of trying to get people to understand this basic fundamental. No, there are only three ways to reap money from your business. You can mix and match them, and they are not necessarily mutually exclusive, but there are only three:

- You sell your business.
- You take cash out of your business. You don't spend it all, but instead save and invest a substantial portion of it.

- You build succession into the business plan so that after a certain period of time you can have somebody else run your business. You don't have to work it, and you still get the benefit of the income from the business.

These techniques can be combined. Let's say a business has maxed out in terms of its value, and that investing more money into it isn't really going to give it a much greater price. Yet it still produces cash—quite a bit of it. We can still take cash out for a period of years if we *stop* investing heavily in the business—and not have the value decrease. You won't get a premium price, but you will have increased the amount that you earned personally because you have taken out extra money over the years.

Another example is a controlled liquidation that is, in fact, a form of selling. It will often give a better return when you have asset-rich companies, such as what you find with machineshop owners or with people who own their own buildings. I presently have a client whose company is worth easily three times more dead than it is alive. Why? Because the building was purchased twenty years ago and is now in a prime location and has a much higher value and better use as a building than as a machine shop, plus they have equipment that was purchased years ago that is paid off and could now be sold.

WHAT IS THE "SECRET DIRTY TRUTH" OF WEALTH CREATION?

The secret is an aggressive retirement savings program starting on Day One, in which you make regular contributions as a mandatory part of doing business. It does not matter how much you put in when you start, say $2,000 a year, but you need to make consistent/regular contributions on a monthly basis if you want to grow your wealth base. In addition to this basic savings program, you'll want to increase that monthly contribution on a yearly basis. This type of savings plan takes discipline, but it soon becomes a habit, and the results become noticeable very quickly.

Set up on day one a plan where you put $100 a month away into a retirement. Have it be an automatic deduction out of your business account, and every year, increase that by 10 percent or something similar. That would be very aggressive planning for a startup. For most people when they're starting up, cash is tight. But if you will get into the habit of saving aggressively, you'll start building assets. The sooner you build assets, the sooner they start accumulating, and the easier it gets.

Now, this next part is important. Take the retirement cash out of your company and invest it. To do so effectively, you must invest in a balanced portfolio of securities, something that is less risky than your business. This may give you less of a return, but it is still going to provide an income.

Please consult your investment advisor regarding potential investment opportunities and strategies.

ARE THERE OTHER IDEAS THAT OWNERS CAN USE TO INCREASE THE ULTIMATE VALUE THEY RECEIVE WHEN THEY EXIT?

1. **Employee Stock Ownership Plans,** also known as ESOPs, are mechanisms that allow employee ownership of a business, either in full or in part. They were developed in the late 1960s in order to create broader ownership of businesses, and there are certain tax advantages that are given to encourage them. ESOPs are fairly complicated, and I suggest strongly that you discuss their advantages with a tax specialist, but here are some examples of their advantages.

ESOPS are like retirement programs, so the payments made to them come out as an expense. You're essentially paying for the purchase of stock with before-tax dollars. This greatly increases the price that can be paid for the company. Here is another provision— under certain circumstances when employees sell their stock to an ESOP, and if they reinvest that money into certain types of securities, then that money will be treated as a tax-deferred exchange, just as if someone was buying your company and paying for it with stock. Another provision that can be an advantage to owners selling through an ESOP is how borrowed money is treated. If you borrow money to fund the purchase of the stock, *both* the principal and the interest can be paid out of pre-tax dollars, not just the interest. This means that a bit more can be paid for the stock of the company.

2. The use of **top-heavy retirement plans** are strong tools for wealth creation. There are ways that you can work within the context of normal retirement laws to your advantage. ERISA, an acronym for Employee Retirement Income Security Act, is a set of laws governing retirement accounts, one of which limits your contributions in a single year. That is why in your ESOP or your 401(k), you are limited to so many dollars that you can put in per year. And the ERISA laws are generally designed to treat all employees fairly, so that even though you're the president/owner of the company, all you can take out under an ERISA plan is in line with your salary.

However, there are ways within the scope of ERISA laws to design plans that will allow you, and the highly-compensated people within the company, to take out much more. That's why I call these plans top-heavy, and I use these plans particularly when I'm trying to help owners who want to retire soon, and who need to build up their retirement assets quickly because they haven't put away enough money.

3. Re-think the **use of cash flow in your business.** The best way to think about your cash flow is to compare it to a company that's growing. If I'm trying to grow my business, I'm saying to myself, "I've got to invest a certain amount of dollars into additional stock, marketing, and physical assets...whatever it is that I need to do to increase my business." And all those investments, in theory, have payoffs down the road in terms of greater sales and, hopefully, greater profits. But...there's an axiom that says that as we grow, we use cash. So, as we're growing, we're hiring more people before the revenue actually builds up; we're increasing our receivables; we're increasing our inventory...*You need to remind yourself that just because you're growing, it doesn't mean you're adding value to your business.*

If you finally get to the point where you are three to five years from looking at your exit, you must take a very hard look at what you are investing in and reevaluate those things, because if they're not increasing value, you're throwing away cash that you could be taking out of your business and investing toward your financial independence.

So take a good, hard look at your growth and tax plans and determine the payoff period on your investments. Consider your targets, with special emphasis on your exit plan. Remember, it's all in the planning.

DOES IT MATTER IF A COMPANY
HAS SUBSTANTIAL DEBT?

Just because a company is highly leveraged with substantial debt, it's not necessarily a bad thing. At some point in time it will certainly hinder your flexibility, vis-a-vis the amount of money you can afford to take out of your business. Instead of panicking, however, reevaluate your model. In the best scenario, e.g., the plan for a growing company, slow down growth for a while. Save the dollars by not hiring any new staff, for instance, and focus on debt repayment. Often, business owners are so concerned about growth they don't look at the other side.

HOW DOES ONE SELL A BUSINESS?

First of all, it depends on the size of the business, because there are different intermediaries who work in different size ranges. If you have a business that is going to sell for, let's say, $1,500,000 or less, it is most likely going to be bought by an individual who wants to run a small business. In that event, you're going to be dealing with a business broker, potentially somebody who is local. You will want to talk to your other trusted advisors—your lawyers, accountants, bankers, insurance representatives—and get names from them.

Depending on the size of the community where you are located, i.e., Los Angeles, you could have hundreds of intermediaries to choose from. If you're in a city the size of Albuquerque, there may be only a few people, and you'll see the same names come up again and again in terms of who are the most competent.

When you start getting into larger transactions, let's say $5,000,000 and over, there is a much smaller cadre of people who do this type of work. Most of those people will have websites and most of them will be on the Internet. Use a search engine such as Google and search for *merger acquisitions intermediary*. Read the websites and see what size ranges the consultant deals with, and then begin a process of telephone interviews and pre-qualification.

Checking references is absolutely critical. When you are taking on a high-level service from a person who is unknown to you, the best way to decide whether you have a good fit for your needs is to get references—a minimum of three, and preferably five or more. Talk to these references and ask them about the person you are considering. Some questions to ask are: Did the person act in a responsible manner and show professionalism? Did the person follow through on promises? Did the person deliver results that were satisfactory to you?

WHAT ARE THE STEPS TO SELLING A BUSINESS?

There are three important steps to selling a business. First, you want your business to be attractive. By being attractive, we mean you want to ensure that you are making money, that you have as little debt as possible, and that your financial records are clean and follow generally accepted accounting principles. Those are the very first preparations an owner should make before selling a business.

Second, if there is time, business owners should make sure that their role in the business is minimized and that other people within the business are carrying out critical activities, whether sales and marketing or operations.

Third, if there is time, I recommend that business owners spend time documenting processes and procedures. With those three steps in place, you should be a reasonably acceptable acquisition candidate.

I would *never* recommend to business owners that they attempt to sell their own business. It is a very time-consuming process to bring a company to market, to screen potential buyers, and figure out who is a qualified buyer. I believe it is money well spent to get a professional with a proven track record in your size business, industry, and region, to bring your business to market. It's the same for selling a house. There are some people who are very successful selling their own homes, but most people find that that it is not a productive use of their time, and that they really don't understand how the market works.

IS THERE AN OVERVIEW OF A
TYPICAL PODOLNY FIRST ENGAGEMENT?

The Podolny Method© begins with an overview of a person's basic values, and the influences that cause him or her to make significant decisions, business or otherwise. I want to know what a person likes or dislikes in the way of work. Do you like managing? Do you like overseeing operations? Do you like selling? Do you dislike finance? Do you dislike people management? Those types of likes and dislikes are very important in determining what somebody is willing and not willing to do in the future of the business.

I want to know what the owners' outside interests are. I want to know what owners have a passion for and what they would like to be doing outside of work. I want to know what's going on in terms of their time. Do they have enough time to pursue both their work and their non-work interests? If there is not enough time, does that mean that there's any kind of resentment? Does that mean that there's any kind of problem, or are they content with the status quo? I want to know what their personal energy level is and what the trend is for that energy level.

I also need to understand their ego goals. We don't like to talk about these, but often those of us who own businesses have something to prove; to others and to ourselves. These realities should not be denied.

Finally, I want a sense—via an objective financial evaluation— of what it's going to take for that person to have financial independence. This is an empirical exercise of going through their expenses, and what they would like to be spending money on when they are no longer working, and then comparing those figures to what they have already saved and what their business is likely to be worth.

When I evaluate the business, I look at all the essential factors that any third party doing an evaluation of the business would look at. *Who do they sell to? How much do they sell? What kind of profit do they make on sales? How do they market? How do they sell? What's their production process? How is it managed and controlled? What kind of physical assets do they have? What kind of asset replacement cycle do they have in place?*

I look at the whole of a client's financial history, and by applying the critical formulas that bankers use in terms of looking at ratios and numbers, I will eventually come to a full evaluation of the business.

Based upon these factors, I will find aspects of the business that are not in harmony. For example, I may find a person who says, "I'm really tired. My energy level's gone." He may love to play more golf or spend more time with his wife, but he needs to realize $5 million from his business in order to achieve financial independence, and his business is worth only $1.5 million.

> *I begin to drive people until they understand what's really critical in achieving their goals and what kind of tradeoffs and decisions are necessary to truly achieve those goals.*

Then I begin to look at the personal and business elements for those interests that are working in opposition to each other, because doing so will tell me where there is opportunity for tangible improvement and change. For example, I might find that the owner is *the* critical element to the company's success, and the only way he can increase the financial value he receives from the business is if he works more. On the other hand, I may find he wants to spend more time with his family and feels burnt out—that's a discontinuity in terms.

I find these types of discontinuities and address them with the owner. Together, we can study the discontinuities, potential tradeoffs, and compromises for resolving them, and what specifically we will need to do to implement the tradeoff or compromise solution. I begin to drive people until they understand what's really critical in achieving their goals and what kind of tradeoffs and decisions are necessary to truly achieve those goals. Then we go about creating an action plan, identifying what it is we need to do, and drawing up the specifics that have to take place in order to achieve those goals.

HOW DO I KNOW IF I SHOULD HIRE A CONSULTANT?

This is an easy one—you should hire a consultant when you are genuinely ready to tackle meaningful change in areas where you lack experience and knowledge. In this book, I have discussed how an owner is a person who has done things his or her own way. They have gone against the "common advice" given.

Yet as the business grows and develops, it cries out for more and more specialized knowledge. "Learning from others' experience and mistakes" can be a very profitable and effective tool. That's what a good consultant should bring to the table; experience and the means to translate it into the circumstances of your business.

HOW DO I CHOOSE AND USE
A CONSULTANT EFFECTIVELY?

As described above regarding choosing an intermediary, talk to a number of consultants. Then check references. When you're ready to move forward, make sure that you are *fully engaged personally in the process!* I have seen many situations where the owner hires a consultant, or agrees to a recommendation from his people to hire one, and then the owner never personally gets involved with the process. These situations never work! The minute the consultant is gone, things go back to the way they were, and no changes are accomplished. You, the owner, must be an active partner in the consulting process.

CHAPTER SIXTEEN

The Podolny Method© Summarized

Why are you in business? What do you expect personally from your business, both now and when your ownership ends and you move on to the next phase of your life?

When a business is being sold, it represents the end of a story. That story is about that owner's life with his business. I designed and perfected The Podolny Method© after spending years assisting owners with the sale of their businesses. I found, more often than not, that my clients were less than satisfied with this final chapter of their story.

It seemed to me almost criminal that so many should be dissatisfied. After all, the business owner is the lynchpin of our private enterprise system. It is the business owner who provides the greatest job growth in our economy, who pays vast amounts of taxes, and who is the primary benefactor of communities, large and small, around our country. Why should he not be reaping the fruits of his labor in terms of personal satisfaction? I decided that my activity in assisting owners to exit from their businesses was coming too late. What was needed was a means to effect change in the basic way that owners perceive of and operate their businesses. This led to The Podolny Method©.

The Podolny Method© is a logical, step-by-step program for initiating real change. First, it helps you determine what you really want. It will help you establish where your business is and how your business works for or against your personal requirements. Most importantly, The Podolny Method© provides you with the tools to initiate and sustain the changes that need to take place if you are to make your business to serve you.

Business owners need to go through some initial planning if they are to end up with a business that is serving them, as opposed to being the servants of their businesses. Once they have the vision of what they want to achieve, they must follow up with a logical means of accomplishing that vision. The Podolny Method© provides business owners with a simple, but powerful, eight-step method for achieving that change.

STEP ONE
Define Your Personal Lifestyle Goals and Career Goals

As business owners, we have two roles that are separate and distinct from our business. The first of these is the quality and substance of our life outside of the business. The other is our career, what we actually spend time doing when at work. Two of the most common frustrations of business owners are that they end up spending more time than they want working in their business, and that they end up doing the tasks on the job that they neither enjoy nor want to be saddled with.

STEP TWO
Define Your Personal Financial Goals

In addition to our use of time and career roles, we also have the role of an investor. As business owners, we are people with an equity interest in a business that represents a substantial portion of our personal net worth. How that asset performs has major implications on our present and future lifestyle.

STEP THREE
Evaluate Your Business

We need to do an objective analysis of our company's operations, cataloging its various functions and evaluating the status of each function as well as the big picture of the competitive environment in which the company operates. We emphasize identify the strengths and weaknesses of our business.

STEP FOUR
Define the Goals of Your Business

Our business operates in an environment outside of us and our personal life. It has customers, suppliers, and employees, all of whom would be affected should our business disappear. Our business operates in a competitive environment and must accomplish certain tasks in order to be successful. What does our business need to do to be a viable competitor? Survival of the business is separate from our own personal goals. Therefore, it is essential to our evaluation to establish goals for the business as a separate entity as if we were not personally involved.

STEP FIVE
Identify and Reconcile Conflicts Between Goals

Steps One through Four identify for us the separate roles and goals that must be accounted for in the planning process. There are almost always conflicts between these goals. These conflicts must be identified. The achievement of some goals is a necessary prerequisite before others can be attained. Reconciliation between goals must be made and a hierarchy of their importance established so that priorities for future action can be defined and adopted.

STEP SIX
Establish Targets

With goals now identified and put into a hierarchy, we can establish our primary and secondary targets—the specific accomplishments that are necessary to achieve the goals. These targets must be defined in terms that can be measured and need to be accomplished within a set period of time.

STEP SEVEN
Develop Action Plans

Finally, we break down the targets into a specific series of actions that will lead to the accomplishment of each target. Now the whole—the goals, targets, and actions—can be assembled into an action plan, a plan that can be used to guide the change desired by the owner.

STEP EIGHT
Initiate and Push Action by Focusing Small

Change is one of the hardest things any organization can seek to achieve. Inertia is a powerful force and is difficult to overcome. One of the keys to the success of The Podolny Method© is its process for creating change. This process is based upon the principle of focusing on small, attainable actions and the use of responsibility, assignments, and deadlines. It is the consistent repetition of this process that will allow you to achieve the change you desire.

For a working sample of The Podolny Method©, see Appendices A and B.

IN SUMMATION

Finally, you are near the end of the book. We have covered many areas, from why a comfortable retirement is not a given result of business ownership to goal-setting, business evaluation, and the ways to really create wealth from your business.

The long-term goal of any business should always relate to how it is going to end...from your personal standpoint as the owner. After working for years in a business, it is perfectly normal for you, the owner, to anticipate some kind of payoff. Specifically, a payoff that will provide you with personal financial security and a good financial rate of return for the risks you have taken. Most owners expect that this goal will be automatically achieved when they sell their business. But, as we have discussed, a sale alone most likely *will not achieve that goal.* Additional financial planning is essential, and the earlier, the better.

If we run our business *as if it needed to be sold at any moment,* a number of productive things will be happening. We will:

1. Pay attention to our finances and financial reporting.
2. Have assurance that we have good management processes and systems in place.
3. Balance our debt load.
4. Watch consciously for the payback we are getting from investments in growth versus the net value of our business.
5. Have a clear focus for our business and be able to verbalize it.

If you are doing all these things regularly, guess what? You will have a remarkably attractive business, a business that *will be very attractive to others* who are in a position to buy your business.

This kind of business is also going to produce profits and surplus cash flow...the kind of cash flow that you can use to build your personal wealth through savings and personal investing.

It will be a business that might also have the kind of people and management depth that would allow you to pursue the succession option.

Utilize this book to your best advantage—put the principles to use. Remember, none of this is theory. Everything presented in this book is practical and based on extensive experience. Using the very same tools presented here has helped many business owners attain their goals. You too can *Make Your Business Worth More to You©*. You too can soon be headed forward on the path to meeting your own goals—via The Podolny Method's© *Shortcut to Security*.

APPENDIX A

SAMPLE

EXIT AND SUCCESION OPTIONS ANALYTICAL REPORT FOR AMORETTO HOLDINGS

The following report has been prepared for AMORETTO HOLDINGS, a fictional entity representing an actual client.[1]

EXIT AND SUCCESION OPTIONS ANALYTICAL REPORT
Presented by *The Podolny Group* for
PETER STUDDARD, MICHAEL PFEFFER,
NEIL BLACK, and AMORETTO HOLDINGS

This report will review the pertinent information we have collected on you and your business. It will discuss the critical issues affecting the ability of your business to serve your personal needs as you have defined them. It will highlight issues that we recommend be resolved and will provide suggestions for paths you may take to better achieve the goals desired.

PERSONAL EVALUATION – MICHAEL

- Michael believes in integrity, doing things the right way, and treating people fairly.
- Lifestyle is important. He is not happy in Santa Fe as the city has developed today. At some point he would like to move, probably within the same timeframe as his exit

---

[1] Names herein have been changed to protect confidentiality.

scenario.
- His work preferences would include CEO, COO, oversight of IT development, teaching, and training.
- He would not like line management, sales, finance, accounting, or HR detail.
- He has many outside interests and feels he has the time to enjoy them.
- Michael's energy level is good, though he is experiencing a natural decline associated with getting old.
- He believes he will have good energy in the future and is looking for new challenges.
- Wealth primarily represents a tool to create lifestyle, but he also considers it as a measure of accomplishment to some degree.
- Exit horizon—three to five years.
- Exit income desired—$100,000.
- This implies gaining $2 million in shareholder value (assuming a 5 percent earning rate), $2.6 million pre-tax (assuming 23 percent federal and state capital gain taxes).

PERSONAL EVALUATION – PETER

- Peter believes in honesty and integrity.
- His family is one of the most important things in his life.
- He derives great enjoyment from what he does at the company.
- His work preferences would include CEO, COO, finance, accounting, and purchasing.
- He would not like line management, customer relations, sales, HR, or IT.
- His family is his major outside activity, along with some sports, such as tennis.
- Peter's energy is good, though somewhat reduced due to his current lifestyle (i.e., young children).
- He feels no conflict between the time requirements of work and the time available for personal activities.
- Peter perceives he will have good energy going forward.

- Wealth represents a tool to create lifestyle.
- Exit horizon—five to ten years.
- Exit income desired—$150,000.
- This implies gaining $3 million in shareholder value (assuming a 5 percent earning rate), $3.9 million pre-tax (assuming 23 percent federal and state capital gain taxes). Peter has accumulated approximately $400,000 toward his goal.

PERSONAL EVALUATION – NEIL

- Neil values work. He is a goal and results-oriented person, as can be observed in his outside interests.
- Long-term security (financial) is extremely important to him.
- His work preferences are CEO, COO, purchasing, line management, and sales.
- He would not like finance, accounting, HR, or IT.
- Neil has substantial outside interests including auto racing, outdoor sports, working out, and travel.
- He feels he has sufficient time to enjoy his outside interests.
- Neil's energy level is good, but he sees it naturally declining.
- He made specific note that he felt he was underutilizing his capabilities and energies.
- Exit horizon—six years.
- Exit income desired—$150,000.
- This implies gaining $3 million in shareholder value (assuming a 5 percent earning rate), $3.9 million pre-tax (assuming 23 percent federal and state capital gain taxes). Neil has accumulated approximately $400,000 toward his goal.

BUSINESS REVIEW

AMORETTO HOLDINGS (AH) is a stable business that has performed at a consistently high financial level, which has translated

into significant cash-on-cash rates of return for its owners. The company operates two distinct concepts:
- Fine dining—the firm's original concepts—consisting of Mazzo and Brubella restaurants.
- Upscale fast casual—the AMORETTO chain.

The AMORETTO concept clearly has the higher capability for leverage (leverage defined as growth and increased shareholder return), due to its price/lifestyle position within the dining market, lower food and labor costs, and an easier ability to replicate the concept.

It should be noted that Mazzo and Brubella, up to the current period, have been extremely important contributors to AH financially, as can be viewed in the Financial Analysis located in Exhibit I at the end of this report. Based upon the three-year period 2004 to 2006, these operations represent 58 percent of the cash flow and estimated market value of the company. This evaluation is subject to change, based upon 2007 numbers, as it has been indicated that both Mazzo and Brubella had weaker performance. Mazzo, in particular, has significant competitive questions, because of the overbuilding in San Diego of chain restaurants and casinos.

The leveraging of the AMORETTO concept is complicated by the AMORETTO International (AVI) situation, with ownership of three locations split with a third party that is no longer a partner AH ownership wishes to continue with and by the disagreement over the ownership of intellectual property.

Company operations appear strongest in the areas of line management, along with operational and quality control systems. Ownership has provided an environment that promotes a quality place to work, leading to low turnover in key positions. However, the strength of marketing, IT, and financial data management are down a level.

The corporate culture has been described by management as "being a pretty good place to work, semi-dynamic, open, and easy-going."

Ownership perceives the company's strengths as:
- The relationship between the owners
- Integrity

- The AMORETTO concept
- Operating systems

It perceives the company's weaknesses as:
- Organization
- Follow-through
- Limited knowledge by the owners vis-a-vis concerning future direction
- Accountability within the organization

Financially, AH is strong in terms of both condition (Balance Sheet) and performance (Income Statement; refer to Financial Analysis in Exhibit I at the end of this report). Margins related to prime costs (food and labor) are excellent by industry averages. This carries over to the firm's overall financial performance, as evidenced by the strength of its historical cash payouts to ownership.

The current estimated market value of AH is substantially less than the amounts that have been targeted by ownership to meet their personal financial targets. When we break down the value of the component pieces of AH, they are essentially the same as the whole. This is positive, as the whole would be difficult to sell because of the differences in the component concepts. There would also be difficulties achieving a full value for the AMORETTO component today because of the AVI situation.

EVALUATION

Overall, there is a single, overriding issue that unavoidably demands attention. How is this ownership group going to achieve the personal financial and exit goals they have established? From a goals and values perspective, the owners, as a group, are fairly homogeneous. There are some differences of timeframe of exit, but no major issues appear in urgent need of reconciliation. There seems to be a desire for a greater challenge, but that is offset by the obvious enjoyment the owners have for their current lifestyle.

AH is a good business with excellent financial performance and strong operational underpinnings. If the owners were content having a business that maintained or gradually improved in market value, there would be no pressing reasons to change. But the indications of the owners are that they wish to earn a valuation that is three to four times greater than it is currently and over a relatively short (five-year) period of time.

What works well for a private owner does not necessarily translate into excellent marketability should owners bring their business to market. If the method to achieve shareholder value is a sale of the business (and note that there are other methods), there are four areas that I believe need attention for the company to significantly increase its value and its marketability.

IT SYSTEMS – The company has excellent operational systems, but lacks a point-of-sale system collecting real-time data that could be used for more sophisticated market analysis. Any sophisticated buyer looking at AMORETTO HOLDINGS as a concept for expansion would discount its value due to this deficiency.

FINANCIAL REPORTING – For internal purposes, the current system of annual financial statements is more than sufficient. However, for the purposes of a quality buyer they are not. A compilation is not acceptable for major acquirers. A review, or better yet an audit, is preferable. Adding substantial footnotes to the statement would answer many questions before they were asked and add credibility to the statements.

CONCEPUTAL CONFUSION – Having two concepts and two separate ownership schemes detracts seriously from anyone acquiring the company as a whole. The simpler, more focused, and easier to understand a business is—as a concept and as an organization—the more attractive it will to be to a potential acquirer.

LEADERSHIP – The phrase you used to describe your organization, a semi-dynamic place to work,. and the lack of clear accountability for top management demonstrated in the functional organization chart are indicators of room for improvement in the area of leadership. AMORETTO HOLDINGS is clearly a good company, a very good company. But if it wants to improve its value three to four times, it needs to be excellent. A commitment by senior management to excellence, a clear vision, and firm targets for performance and accountability are all components of excellent management.

RECOMMENDATIONS

To achieve the owners' personal financial goals, shareholder value must increase three to four times. If the owners truly wish to achieve their personal financial goals within the timeframe of their exit goals, the company must focus religiously on the building of shareholder value. This will require a real commitment from the owners. A commitment of this nature will have effects on how the business is run, the roles the owners adopt within the business, and potentially the lifestyle of the owners during the period of building shareholder value. These issues need to be seriously contemplated by each owner as we explore the various options for achieving their personal financial and exit goals.

EXAMPLES OF OPTIONS

There are a multitude of variations among the options, with a range of tradeoffs. Some options can be combined. Most will require the same initial steps, meaning the owners do not have to make an irrevocable decision at this time. Below is a sampling of options that will begin to give you an idea of the range available to you.

FULL LEVERAGING OF THE
AMORETTO HOLDINGS CONCEPT

Turn AMORETTO HOLDINGS into a high-growth company that will be valued on its trend rather than the historical average of its financial performance, leading to a higher multiple paid on a larger company.

- A major commitment to upgrading systems is required.
- Growth will need to be consistent and in the 15 to 20 percent annual range.
- Substantial capital will be required to fund growth. This will most likely severely limit the ability to make cash payouts to ownership.
- Redeployment of Mazzo and Brubella assets are likely required to fund growth.
- Owners will be required to put maximum energies into the business.

OPTIMIZED GROWTH WITH FOCUS ON CASH FLOW

Develop a balanced strategic focus that continues growth, but allows for continued cash payouts to shareholders that should be used for investment for exit purposes.

- Improve leadership, and systems to maximize earnings and cash flow potential.
- Use cash payouts to the owners for personal investments that will build the financial worth of each shareholder.
- Consider redeploying assets (Mazzo and/or Brubella) to fund AMORETTO HOLDINGS growth.
- Increase size and value with gradual growth.
- Derive total shareholder value from the growth of the invested cash payouts plus the exit value of the business.

SUCCESSION

Develop the same strategic focus as above, but instead of an exit, develop a management team that can run the business for the owners.

- Improve leadership, and systems to maximize earnings and cash flow potential.
- Use cash payouts to the owners for personal investments that will build the financial worth of each shareholder.
- Consider redeploying assets (Mazzo and/or Brubella) to fund AMORETTO HOLDINGS growth.
- Increase size and value with gradual growth.
- Develop a management team that has the ability to replicate the roles of the current ownership, in both tangible skills and intangible leadership qualities (see Podolny Group website at www. podolny.com for various articles related to business succession on the Newsletters page).
- Total shareholder value derives from the growth of invested cash payouts plus the continuation of cash payouts going forward.

NEXT STEPS

A full understanding of the implications of any option is a requirement for you to make an intelligent decision. Fortunately, as stated above, I believe certain actions are common to most of the options you will want to contemplate. We discussed some of these at our last meeting and included actions related to leadership, corporate vision, and accountability.

We should engage in an in-depth discussion of your options to clarify their individual requirements. I would strongly advise that you include your other long-term advisors in this discussion process. The discussion process needs to lead to a consensus among you and a commitment to action, if it is to achieve the desired results you seek.

EXHIBIT I
FINANCIAL ANALYSIS
AMORETTO HOLDINGS (Consolidated)   '00's Omitted

YEAR	2004	2005	2006	Average
Sales – Amoretto	$4,221	$4,588	$5,128	$4,646
Sales – Mazzo	2,412	2,442	2,277	2,377
Sales – Brubella	2,498	2,764	2,703	2,655
SALES - TOTAL	$9,131	$9,794	$10,108	$9,678
Gross Profit – Amoretto	$1,697	$1,888	$2,373	$1,986
Gross Profit – Mazzo	940	895	809	881
Gross Profit – Brubella	1,007	1,141	1,075	1,074
GROSS PROFIT - TOTAL[2]	$3,644	$3,924	$4,257	$3,942
Gross Margin – Amoretto	40.20%	41.15%	46.28%	42.75%
Gross Margin – Mazzo	38.97%	36.65%	35.53%	37.08%
Gross Margin – Brubella	40.31%	41.28%	39.77%	40.46%
GROSS MARGIN – TOTAL	39.91%	40.07%	42.12%	40.73%
IBT – Amoretto	$211	$209	$171	$197
IBT – Mazzo	51	29	(40)	13
IBT – Brubella	66	70	(43)	31
INCOME BEFORE TAXES – TOTAL	$328	$308	$88	$241
Depreciation – Amoretto	$113	$104	$107	$108
Depreciation – Mazzo	26	27	43	32
Depreciation – Brubella	14	14	15	14
DEPRECIATION – TOTAL	$153	$145	$165	$154
Interest – Amoretto	$33	$33	$28	$31
Interest – Mazzo	0	0	0	0
Interest – Brubella	0	0	0	0
INTEREST – TOTAL	$33	$33	$28	$31
IBITDA – Amoretto	$357	$346	$306	$336
IBITDA – Mazzo	77	56	3	45
IBITDA – Brubella	80	84	(28)	45

---

[2] Gross Profit in the food service industry is commonly defined as Sales less "Prime Costs," which are comprised of Food Costs and Labor

IBITDA – TOTAL	$514	$486	$281	$427
Surplus Owner Comp – Amoretto[3]	$255	$453	$453	$387
ADJUSTED IBITDA TOTAL	$769	$939	$734	$814

Enterprise Value[4] of Total @ 4 times IBITDA	**$3,256**
Less 23% Taxes	749
Net to Shareholders	$2,507

Net Value to Each AH Shareholder	**$836**

Enterprise Value of Total @ 4.5 times IBITDA	**$3,663**
Less 23% Taxes	842
Net to Shareholders	$2,821

Net Value to Each AH Shareholder	**$940**

Mazzo – Separate Valuation

	2004	2005	2006	Average
IBITDA	$77	$56	$3	$45
Plus 50% Corp OH	115	109	102	109
Plus Surplus Corp OH	0	19	16	12
Adj. IBITDA	$192	$184	$121	$166

Enterprise Value of Total @ 4 times IBITDA	**$663**
Less 23% Taxes	152
Net to Shareholders	$510

Net Value to Each Mazzo Shareholder	**$170**

Enterprise Value of Total @ 4.5 times IBITDA	**$746**
Less 23% Taxes	171
Net to Shareholders	$574

Net Value to Each Mazzo Shareholder	**$191**

---

[3] Bonuses

[4] Enterprise Value is before debt adjustment. Any existing debt carried by the business is normally subtracted from enterprise value.

Brubella – Separate Valuation

	2004	2005	2006	Average
IBITDA	$80	$84	($28)	$45
Plus 50% Corp OH	114	124	122	120
Plus Surplus Corp OH	76	155	193	141
Adj. IBITDA	$270	$363	$287	$307

Enterprise Value of Total @ 4 times IBITDA	$1,227
Less 23% Taxes	282
Net to Shareholders	$945

Net Value to Each Brubella Shareholder	**$315**

Enterprise Value of Total @ 4.5 times IBITDA	$1,380
Less 23% Taxes	317
Net to Shareholders	$1,063

Net Value to Each Brubella Shareholder	**$354**

Amoretto - Separate Valuation

	2004	2005	2006	Average
Total Adj. IBITDA	$769	$939	$734	$814
less Mazzo Adj IBITDA	192	184	121	166
less Brubella Adj IBITDA	270	363	287	307
Ind. Adj. IBITDA	$307	$392	$326	$342

Enterprise Value of Total @ 4 times IBITDA	$1,367
Less 23% Taxes	314
Net to Shareholders	$1,052

Net Value to Each Amoretto Shareholder	**$351**

Enterprise Value of Total @ 4.5 times IBITDA	$1,538
Less 23% Taxes	354
Net to Shareholders	$1,184

Net Value to Each Amoretto Shareholder	**$395**

APPENDIX B

SAMPLE

SHORTCUT TO SECURITY IMPLEMENTATION OUTLINE FOR AMORETTO HOLDINGS

I. GOALS

A. *Personal income, post-ownership, and/or active management of $150,000 per annum by 2014*

B. *Define personal highest level of accomplishment goal by 12/31/2011*

II. INTERMEDIATE GOALS

A. *Fill in gaps in professional skill set*

B. *Establish clear leadership and direction within AMORETTO HOLDINGS and its affiliated entities*

C. *Upgrade corporate capabilities*

D. *Establish shareholder value growth strategy*

E. *Create individual shareholder savings plan*

III. IMPLEMENTATION ACTION PLAN

A. *Fill in gaps of professional skill set*
   1. Upgrade management skills of the three principals:

      a. Communication
      b. Leadership
      c. Control and accountability
      d. Planning
      e. Staffing
      f. Problem-solving and decision-making
      g. Time management

   2. Increase knowledge of marketing (see marketing and POS below)

   3. Increase knowledge of CFO functions (see Finance below)

B. *Establish clear leadership and direction within AMORETTO HOLDINGS and its affiliated entities*

   1. Define specific responsibilities for each of the principals:

      a. Job definitions
      b. Create measurable goals for each job
      c. Create accountability systems

   2. Focus the organization

      a. Create a message that conveys the focus you want for yourself and your company
      b. Communicate the message to the organization and imbed it in written and verbal company communications

    c. Push goal-setting down into the organization

    d. Set up accountability systems within the organization that tie into goal-setting

C. *Upgrade corporate capabilities*

   1. Marketing:

      a. Determine data categories important for the expansion of the AMORETTO concept

      b. Research sources of data sought

      c. Collect data

      d. Analyze data

   2. Point-of-sale technology, systems and use

      a. Research available POS systems

      b. Capabilities

      c. What information can they provide that you can use for marketing?

      d. Cost/Benefit analysis

      e. Decision—go/no go/go later

      f. If go, create implementation plan

   3. Finance

      a. Determine functions of an internal finance department

      b. Learn about how the financial world looks at financial statements

      c. Determine potential changes to internal financial functions and financial statements

      d. Decision—go/no go/go later

      e. If go, create implementation plan

D. *Establish shareholder value growth strategy*

   1. Revisit strategic options

      a. Grow AMORETTO HOLDINGS – rapidly, controlled
      b. Sell mature AMORETTO HOLDINGS subdivisions while developing new ones
      c. Franchising
      d. Cash cow, use expertise to do other food-service related options

   2. Cost/Benefit analysis

   3. Decide on a strategy

   4. Create implementation plan

   5. Execute implementation plan

E. *Create individual shareholder savings plan*

   1. Research qualified and non-qualified plans for taking cash out of AMORETTO HOLDINGS

   2. Research available asset managers

   3. Decide

   4. Implement

APPENDIX C

SAMPLE

SHORTCUT TO SECURITY
FINANCIAL INDEPENDENCE
REQUIREMENTS SPREADSHEET

Knowing the amount of income required to support your desired lifestyle is of the utmost importance. We use your annual income requirement as we evaluate the target amount of accumulated funds that you will need to support your lifestyle. This target accumulation amount is a key component of the process we undertake in determining how to *Make Your Business Worth More to You©*. The Podolny Group has created the following, simple spreadsheet to help you calculate the income required to support your desired lifestyle upon reaching financial independence.

The Podolny Group provides this analysis combined with evaluations of your business value and marketability.

For more information contact info@podolny.com.

Instructions: Calculate the amount required for each of the expenditure classes in the chart using the explanation given. In some cases it may be easier to calculate or estimate either an annual amount or a monthly amount, so there are columns for both. Convert all monthly amounts to annual amounts, and then total the annual column.

	Monthly Amount	Annual Amount
Years to Financial Independence[1] =		
Housing – Purchase[2]		
Housing – Maintenance[3]		
Auto – Purchase[4]		
Auto – Maintenance[5]		
Food[6]		
Entertainment[7]		
Medical – Insurance[8]		
Medical - Out of Pocket		
Other – Insurance[9]		
Travel – Vacations[10]		
Clothing		
Education[11]		
Furniture		
Telephone, Computer & Technology[12]		
Legacy & Gifts[13]		
Other – List[14]		
Total Expenditures		
Tax Rate		
Pre-tax Income Target[15]		

1. **Years to Financial Independence:** Determine how long it will be from now to when you no longer want to have to work. Calculate this in terms of years from the present.

2. **Housing – Purchase:** Determine if you will have house payments remaining at the time you seek financial independence (as stated above). Enter that payment amount. If you plan to purchase a new home in the future, account for this purchase in the calculation.

3. **Housing – Maintenance:** Utilities, landscape maintenance, pool maintenance, and improvements. Estimate all the maintenance required, both annual and occasional. For example, if you must put a new roof in every ten years, calculate that amount and come up with a monthly or annual amount to add to the maintenance amount. Include homeowner's insurance.

4. **Auto – Purchase:** Based upon your personal auto-buying patterns or desires, figure how often you will buy a new vehicle and the amount you will spend. Assume you will have to pay for this personally, outside the business. Convert into an annual or monthly amount.

5. **Auto – Maintenance:** Gas, oil, insurance, parking, tolls, car washes, and also the maintenance expenses such as tires and tune-ups. Convert to a monthly or annual amount.

6. **Food:** Groceries and dining-out expenses.

7. **Entertainment:** Include any and all forms of entertainment you enjoy and expect to continue in retirement. (Golf, tennis, theater, movies, cable TV, country club, sports, clubs, hobbies, etc.)

8. **Medical Insurance:** Assume you will have to pay for medical insurance now that there is no business to pick up the cost. Take into account that insurance costs have increased much greater than the rate of inflation.

9. **Insurance – Other:** All life insurance, disability, long-term care, etc. (do not include homeowner's and auto insurance, which were included
in previous categories).

10. **Travel – Vacations:** Even if your big vacations aren't every year, convert the amounts you expect to spend into annual amounts.

11. **Education:** College expense, if any is still expected during retirement.

12. **Telephone, Computer, and Technology:** Cell phones, landline telephones, Internet access expenses, computer expenses, home theater electronics, etc.

13. **Legacy and Gifts:** If you plan to create an estate for your heirs, create an annualized amount you expect to leave, in addition to any gifts given during the year.

14. **Other – List:** Any other expenses not covered above.

15. **Pre-tax Income Target:** To determine this amount, do the following calculation:

Total Expenditures / (1.00 – tax rate) = Pre-tax Income Target
Example with a 25 percent tax rate and $100,000 requirement:
$100,000 / (1.00 - .25) = $133.333

List the Life Insurance, disability insurance, and long-term care insurance you are carrying:

List your current retirement and liquid asset savings.

APPENDIX D

GLOSSARY OF TERMS

ERISA (Acronym) – Employee Retirement Income Security Act. U.S. federal statute which sets minimum standards for pension plans in private industry, and provides for extensive rules on Federal income tax effects of dealings in connection with various employee benefit plans. ERISA was enacted to protect interstate commerce and the interests of participants in employee benefit plans and their beneficiaries by requiring the disclosure and reporting to participants and beneficiaries of financial and other information with respect thereto, by establishing standards of conduct, responsibility, and obligation for fiduciaries of employee benefit plans and by providing for appropriate remedies, sanctions, and ready access to the Federal courts.

ESOP (Acronym) – Employee Stock Ownership Plan. An employee benefit plan, which makes the employees of a company also owners of stock in that company. Several features make ESOPs unique compared to other employee benefit plans. First, only an ESOP is required by law to invest primarily in the securities of the sponsoring employer. Second, an ESOP is unique among qualified employee benefit plans in its ability to borrow money. As a result, "leveraged ESOPs" may be used as a technique of corporate finance.

IBITDA (Acronym) – Income Before Interest, Taxes, Depreciation, and Amortization (also known as EBITDA — Earnings Before Interest, Taxes, Depreciation, and Amortization). IBITDA differs from the operating cash flow in a cash flow statement primarily by excluding payments for taxes or interest, as well as changes in working capital. IBITDA also differs from free cash flow, because it excludes cash requirements for replacing capital assets. IBITDA is used when evaluating a company's ability to earn a profit, and it is often used in stock analysis.

APPENDIX E

CONTACT AND BOOKING

For more information on The Podolny Method©, or to receive a no-cost, no-obligation evaluation of your business and your personal goals, contact:

THE PODOLNY GROUP, INC.

HEADQUARTERS
2108 White Cloud NE
Albuquerque, NM 87112
505.856.2646

LOS ANGELES

CHICAGO

www.podolny.com
info@podolny.com

Michael Podolny is available for speaking engagements. If you would like to book Michael to speak to your business or group, please contact 505.856.2646 or email info@podolny.com

ABOUT MICHAEL PODOLNY

Michael Podolny has specialized in issues affecting private business owners for over thirty years, beginning his career as a commercial lender serving middle-sized businesses and initiating over $150 million in financing. While at First National Bank of Maryland he created *FirstList*, a publication that connected acquisition, financing and equity capital seekers and sources. *FirstList* remains a mainstay of the middle market merger/acquisition industry.

Michael was a major contributor to the highly acclaimed reference books *How To Do A Leverage Buyout*, *The Directory of Financing Sources* and *The Directory of Intermediaries*. He was also a principal contributor to *The Journal of Buyouts and Acquisitions* and a speaker in the national seminar series, *How To Do A Leveraged Buyout*.

As a founding shareholder in Sirrah Corporation, a Chicago based merger/acquisition intermediary, and eventual managing director of the firm, Michael worked with hundreds of business owners, representing them in the search for business combination partners, recapitalizations, and debt and equity financing. Michael initiated and closed transactions with an aggregate value exceeding $200 million while at Sirrah Corporation.

Over time he recognized that investment banking transactions were extremely limited. They only could resolve a small portion of business ownership issues that were the root of the business owners' decision to sell. Michael researched and found that there were a set of personal/individual variables that need to be included in any business planning process if an owner was to get their desired outcome. He developed a proprietary method to assist business owners with reconciling personal and business issues quickly and efficiently then putting into action the changes necessary to achieve the desired results.

Moving to Albuquerque, New Mexico he founded The Podolny Group in 1993 based upon these principles. Today the Podolny Group serves business owners around the country to make the businesses worth more and run better. The firm has offices in Chicago, IL and Los Angeles, CA as well as its headquarters in Albuquerque.

ABOUT JOEL EISENBERG

Joel Eisenberg is a filmmaker and author, whose best-selling motivational book about the creative process, *How to Survive a Day Job*, was followed in December 2008 by *You're Too Smart to Go Down Stupid*. Eisenberg made headline news in 2007 by locating, identifying, organizing, and archiving a long-considered lost John Steinbeck archive. He is presently developing a feature film based on the life of publishing magnate William M. Gaines. Joel's work has been covered extensively via numerous outlets, including CBS, NBC, FOX, ABC, MSNBC, the *Los Angeles Daily News*, the *Los Angeles Times*, *TV Guide*, as well as internationally.